Ethiopian Scribal Practice 1

Ethiopic Manuscript Imaging Project

Ethiopic Manuscripts, Texts, and Studies

Series Editor
Steve Delamarter

Forthcoming volumes

Veronika Six, Getatchew Haile, Melaku Terefe, Jeremy R. Brown, Erik C. Young, and Steve Delamarter. *Catalogue of the Ethiopic Manuscript Imaging Project: Volume 2, Codices 106–200 and Magic Scrolls 135–284.*

Steve Delamarter and Melaku Terefe. *Ethiopian Scribal Practice 2: Plates for the Catalogue of the Ethiopic Manuscript Imaging Project* (Companion to EMIP Catalogue 2).

Getatchew Haile, Melaku Terefe, Jeremy R. Brown, Erik C. Young and Steve Delamarter. *Catalogue of the Ethiopic Manuscript Imaging Project: Volume 3, Codices 201–300 and Magic Scrolls 286 ff.*

Steve Delamarter and Melaku Terefe. *Ethiopian Scribal Practice 3: Plates for the Catalogue of the Ethiopic Manuscript Imaging Project* (Companion to EMIP Catalogue 3).

Getatchew Haile, Melaku Terefe, Jeremy R. Brown, Erik C. Young and Steve Delamarter. *Catalogue of the Ethiopic Manuscript Imaging Project: Volume 4, Codices 301–400 and Magic Scrolls.*

Steve Delamarter and Melaku Terefe. *Ethiopian Scribal Practice 4: Plates for the Catalogue of the Ethiopic Manuscript Imaging Project* (Companion to EMIP Catalogue 4).

Ethiopian Scribal Practice 1

Plates for the Catalogue of
the Ethiopic Manuscript Imaging Project

Steve Delamarter and Melaku Terefe

Companion to EMIP Catalogue 1

☙PICKWICK *Publications* · Eugene, Oregon

ETHIOPIAN SCRIBAL PRACTICE 1
Plates for the Catalogue of the Ethiopic Manuscript Imaging Project

Ethiopic Manuscripts, Texts, and Studies 2

Copyright © 2009 Steve Delamarter. All rights reserved. Except for brief quotations in critical publications or reviews, no part of this book may be reproduced in any manner without prior written permission from the publisher. Write: Permissions, Wipf and Stock Publishers, 199 W. 8th Ave., Suite 3, Eugene, OR 97401.

Pickwick Publications
A Division of Wipf and Stock Publishers
199 W. 8th Ave., Suite 3
Eugene, OR 97401

ISBN13: 978-1-60608-872-2

Cataloging-in-Publication data:

Delamarter, Steve.
    Ethiopian scribal practice 1 : plates for the catalogue of the Ethiopic Manuscript Imaging Project / Steve Delamarter and Melaku Terefe.

        p. ; cm. —Includes 116 plates, bibliographic references, and indexes.

    Ethiopic Manuscripts, Texts, and Studies 2

    ISBN 13: **978-1-60608-872-2**

    Note: Companion to EMIP Catalogue 1

    1. Codicology. 2. Manuscripts—Ethiopic—Catalogs. 3. Scribes—Ethiopian. 4. Scribes—Africa. I. Terefe, Melaku. II. Title. III. Series.

    BS4.5 E75 v. 2

Manufactured in the U.S.A.

Cover art: EMIP 44 (Eliza Codex 19), f. 140v, closeup of *haräg*; a 20th century Psalter, perhaps made in the Government scriptorium.

To my friends and colleagues at the Institute of Ethiopian Studies

Contents

Series Foreword / ix
Abbreviations / xi
Preface / xiii
Introduction / xv

Description and Analysis of Scribal Practices with Plates / 1

List of the Manuscripts by EMIP and Owner Number / 179
List of Dated or Datable Manuscripts by Date / 181
List of Undated Manuscripts by Date / 183
For Further Reading / 185
Index of Scribal Practices / 193

Series Foreword

The series *Ethiopic Manuscripts, Texts, and Studies* offers, in the first place, catalogues of the Ethiopic Manuscript Imaging Project whose purpose it is to digitize and catalogue collections of Ethiopic manuscripts in North America and around the world. Beyond this, though, the series offers a venue for monographs, revised dissertations, and texts that explore the rich historical, literary, and artistic traditions of Ethiopia and the Ethiopian Orthodox Church.

    The series has particular interest in Ethiopic manuscripts and the scribal practices in evidence within them. This includes analytical studies of particular manuscripts or particular scribal practices and illuminations. Moreover, the interest extends to synthetic studies that explore the developments of scribal and artistic practice across time or those that probe the interconnections between common elements in manuscripts, scribal practices, scribal education, and community ideology.

Steve Delamarter, series editor

Abbreviations

BIE = Sergew Hable Selassie, *Bookmaking in Ethiopia*. Leiden: Karstens Drukkers, 1981.

MP Scribes = Mellors, John and Anne Parsons. *Scribes of South Gondar*. London: New Cross Books, 2002.

MP Bookmaking = Mellors, John and Anne Parsons. *Ethiopian Bookmaking*. London: New Cross Books, 2002.

PPM = Assefa Liben, "Preparation of Parchment Manuscripts." *Bulletin of Ethnological Museum, University College of Addis Ababa* 8 (1958) 254–267.

Preface

My personal starting point for the study of Ethiopic manuscripts was the study of the Dead Sea Scrolls. More specifically, it was the strand of Emmanuel Tov's work that culminated in his *Scribal Practices and Approaches Reflected in the Texts Found in the Judean Desert* (Brill, 2004). To the interests raised in Tov's work, I overlaid the sociological models and sensitivities evidenced in the work of Shemaryahu Talmon. This convinced me of the need for more robust (i.e., sociologically informed) models of scribal practice. This in turn led to a period of study of the works of medieval codicologists, particularly those involved in the so-called New Codicology. An absolute masterpiece in this regard is Michelle P. Brown's *The Lindisfarne Gospels: Society, Spirituality and the Scribe.* (The British Library Studies in Medieval Culture; London: British Library, 2003). From these works I have developed an intense interest in scribal practice and bible-making communities. This is, perhaps, the distinctive interest that I bring to this project to catalogue and study Ethiopic manuscripts.

Several times a week, *Kesis* Melaku Terefe and I work together by means of video conferencing (Skype). In recent months we have been completing the manuscripts content portion of the catalogue entries for volumes two, three and four in this series of catalogues of the Ethiopic Manuscript Imaging Project. Professor Getatchew played the central and detailed role in the cataloguing of volume one, both in reference to the codices and the magic scrolls. In volume two, Dr. Veronika Six is the primary scholar with reference to the magic scrolls and Professor Getatchew has reviewed with me all of the codices in volumes two and three, making initial determinations about content and final decisions about dating. But in the case of these more recent volumes it has been left to *Kesis* Melaku and me to work through the manuscripts and complete, in detail, the catalogue entries—all under the watchful supervision of Professor Getatchew. And at every point along the way, I and my students have been the ones to tend to the description of the scribal practices in evidence in the manuscripts. Initially Roger Rundell was central to this work; more recently it is Jeremy Brown and Erik Young.

The current volume, with its attention to details of scribal practice, is an expression of this central interest of my scholarship and of my approach to the Ethiopic manuscript tradition. My ongoing cataloguing with *Kesis*

Melaku has informed so many details of my understanding along the way that he is justly listed as an author along with me.

Once again I wish to acknowledge the generosity of the owners who have made their manuscripts available to us for digitizing and research. For this volume these include (in chronological order): Paul Herron (of Oregon), Eliza Bennett (of Colorado), Blake and Claire Marwick (of Oregon), Mr. Whisnant of Louisiana), Shepherd and Sharon Earl (of Oregon), Trinity Western University (British Columbia, Canada), Lee Kirk (acting on behalf of the Tsunami bookshop in Oregon), Hazel Kahan (of New York), Luigi Focanti (of Utah), University of Oregon Museum of Natural and Cultural History (of Oregon), Mount Angel Seminary Library (of Oregon), Gerald Weiner (of Illinois), Theodore Bernhardt (of New Jersey), and Abilene Christian University (of Texas). The reader can consult the introduction to the catalogue volume for more information about the history of the Ethiopic Manuscript Imaging Project.

I want to express again what I have already expressed at some length elsewhere: the extent of my gratitude and learning from other scholars who have introduced me to this or that matter of Ethiopian Studies, These include Professor Getatchew Haile, Professor Richard Pankhurst, *Ato* Demeke Berhane, Dr. Veronika Six, *Ato* Fentahun Tiruneh and (more recently) Professor Lucas Van Rompay.

Steve Delamarter
Pentecost, 2009

Introduction

This book is the companion volume to the *Catalogue of the Ethiopic Manuscript Imaging Project, Volume 1: Codices 1–105, Magic Scrolls 1–134*. It contains at least one plate for each of the 105 codices described in that volume. But this is designed to be more than just a "plates volume." We have selected images from the various manuscripts to tell a host of stories about Ethiopic manuscripts:
- cases (single and double-slip),
- covers and coverings (including leather and cloth),
- the tooling of leather covers,
- layout of text on the page (with prickings, columns and scored lines),
- codex binding (including primary binding chain stitches and secondary fixing points with headband and tail band),
- the marking of content divisions,
- iconography and illuminations,
- the dating of manuscripts (with colophons and other references to historical persons as well as through an analysis of the paleography),
- mirrors and mirror niches in the inside covers of books,
- navigation systems (including strings sewn in the fore edge of books),
- forged paintings,
- quire numbers,
- arranging of contents (for days of the week, church year, etc.),
- the standard formatting of standard works (Psalters, Homiliaries, Missals),
- dimensions of books and how they change across time,
- repairs (to folios, quires, bindings, boards),
- explanations of genres,
- methods for dating of manuscripts,
- musical notation,
- quire construction (including the use of half sheets),
- the use of red ink (names, full-stop symbols, full lines as section divisions, etc.),
- marks of ownership (including seals),
- the completion of long lines of text in Psalters,
- protection sheets,

- the use of rejected sheets from other manuscripts,
- the social location of different grades of codices,
- composite codices (made of quires from differing dates),
- the characteristics of deluxe manuscripts,
- columetric layout of text (especially in Psalms 135, 150 and in the tenth biblical canticle),
- notes, records and other information in the end leaves of books,
- scribal training and apprenticeship,
- scribal systems for the insertion of overlooked material,
- magical prayers (*asmat*), incantations and palindromes,
- marking the midpoint of the Psalms,
- colored fabric lining the inside of wooden covers with leather covering,
- "accordion-fold" codices,
- amulet codices,
- spine straps,
- damage (from water and animals that eat the pages),
- the treatment of the spiritual meanings of the Hebrew Letters in Psalm 118 (= ET 119),
- Ethiopian Manuscript Microfilm Library (EMML) manuscripts come to North America,
- bugs trapped in books, and
- marginal commentaries.

Thus, this book is a work on the practices of Ethiopian scribes. It represents a first installment on the way toward a comprehensive treatment of the subject which we shall attempt when we have completed the cataloguing of the manuscripts.

All of these images, along with the other tens of thousands of images of the Ethiopic Manuscript Imaging project, are available online at the website of the Hill Museum and Manuscript Library, found at http://www.hmml.org/vivarium/sgd.htm.

Description and Analysis of Scribal Practices with Plates

Plate 1: EMIP 1 (Herron Codex), codex and case

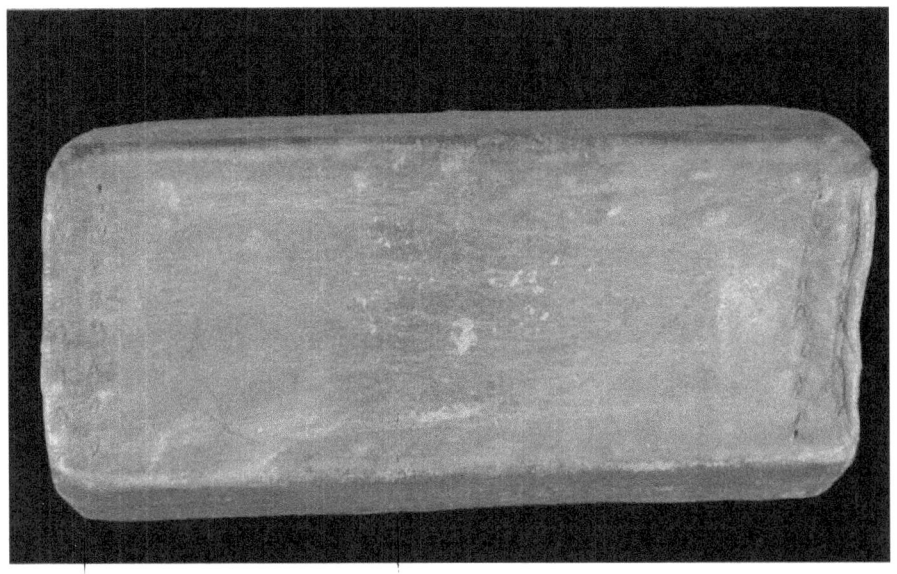

Plate 2: EMIP 2 (Eliza Codex 1), spine with stitching for head and tail bands

Plate 1: EMIP 1—The Herron Codex

This Psalter, copied in the late 17th century, was, at some point, owned by the monastery of Däbrä Gännät (ff. 176v–177r). In this image, the codex, spine side showing, sits in the inner case of the double-slip *maḥdar*. The outer case slides over the top of the inner case and, when carried upright, protects the codex from rain.[1]

Plate 2: EMIP 2—Eliza Codex 1

This 18th-century Psalter, was sold, at some point, for ten Bərr (in 2009 this would be just about equal to one U. S. dollar). In this image, the codex, sitting on its fore edge, shows the spine with stitching near top and bottom for securing the head and tail bands.

---

[1] Sergew (*BIE*, pp. 26-27) discusses the possible dates of origin of these cases in Ethiopia.

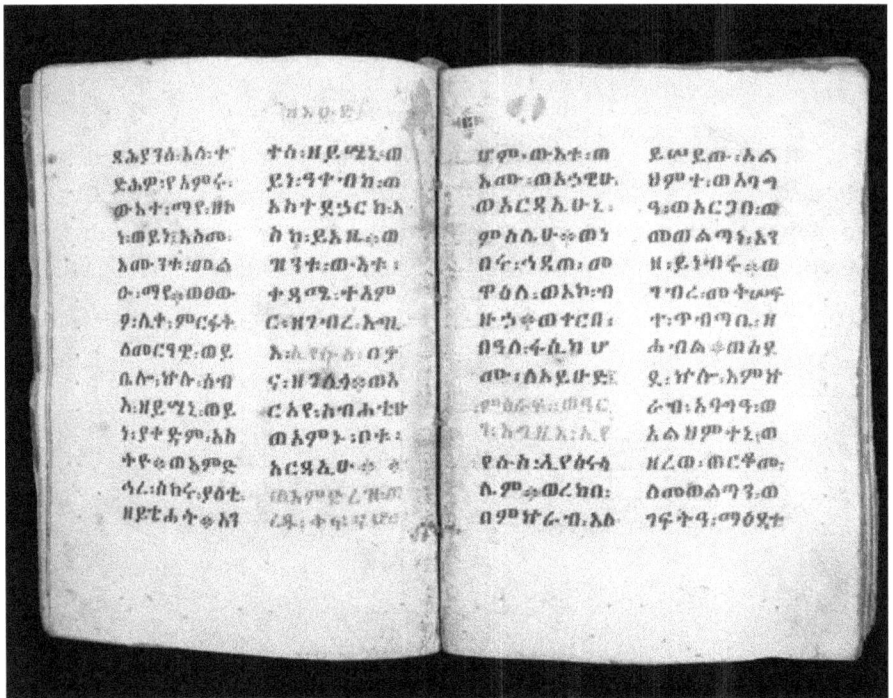

Plate 3: EMIP 3 (Eliza Codex 2), ff. 8v–9r

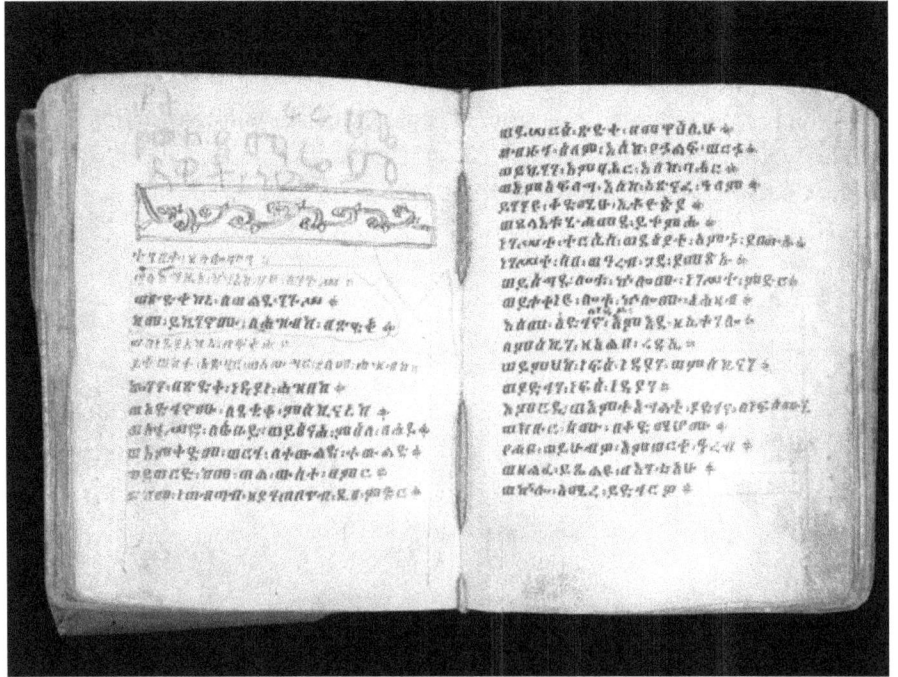

Plate 4: EMIP 4 (Eliza Codex 3), ff. 61r–62v

Plate 3: EMIP 3—Eliza Codex 2

This manuscript was copied in the late 20th century and contains the Gospel of John in ff. 1r–111v. Two smaller works, Prayer of the Covenant (ff. 112r–121v) and Image of Mary's Assumption (ff. 121v–126r) are also included. This image shows many things: the name of Jesus in red ink (f. 8v, column 2, line 8), the day of the week on which this section was to be read (in red ink above column two), the gutter between two quires (the four chain stitches of the binding are visible), a quire number in the upper left corner of folio 9r, prickings on both left and right folios.[2]

Plate 4: EMIP 4—Eliza Codex 3

Copied in the 20th century, this codex contains 17 *harägoč* (plural of *haräg*), colorful vine-like patterns, to designate section divisions in the Psalter. Scribal practice observes up to 19 divisions: 15 in the psalms (one for every ten psalms), one between the Psalms and the Biblical Canticles, one between Biblical Canticles and Song of Songs, one at the head of Praises of Mary, and (occasionally) one between Praises of Mary and Gate of Light. This particular image shows the division at Psalm 61. The old Ethiopian numbering system, which lacks a zero, sees divisions not between numbers ending in 9 and zero, but between numbers designating tens (e.g., 10, 20, 30, 40, etc.) and one (e.g., 11, 21, 31, 41, etc.). This image also shows the center of a quire and the strings used to secure the main binding of the codex (mid-top and mid-bottom) and those used to secure the top and bottom of the quires to the head and tail bands (very top and very bottom).

---

[2] *PPM*, pp, 260-61, describes the tools and processes for pricking holes in the parchment.

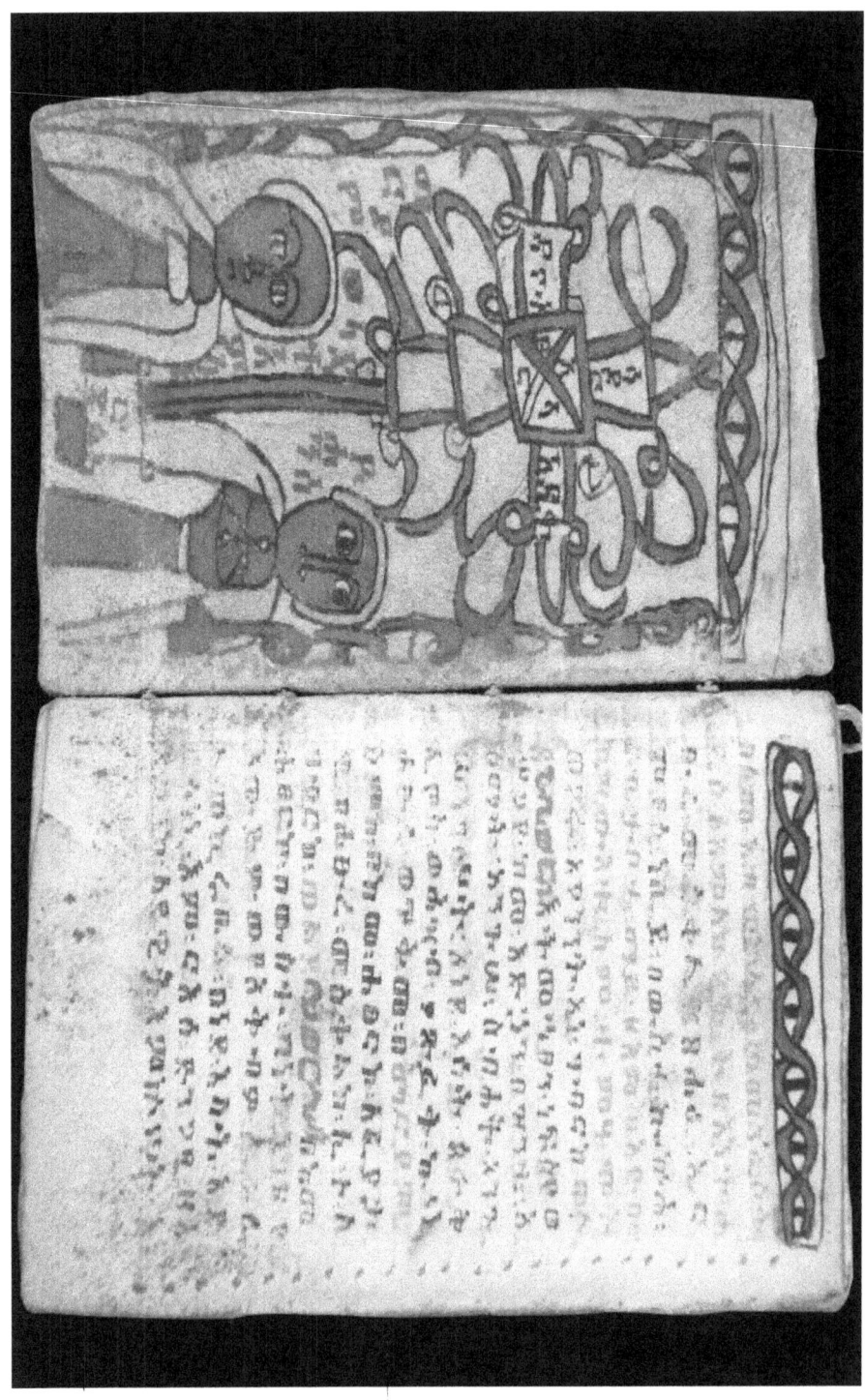

Plate 5: EMIP 5 (Marwick Codex 1), ff. ii v(erso)–1r

Plate 5: EMIP 5—Marwick Codex 1

Copied in the 19th or 20th century, this small codex is made of only 38 folios in four quires. It contains a series of prayers against evil spirits, the second of which (ff. 11r–26v) is a prayer for protection with the power of the cross of Christ. The illumination on f. iiv(erso) is akin to one of the most common icons in Ethiopian Christianity, the scene of the crucifixion with Mary, Jesus' Mother, on the left and the apostle John on the right. The standard icon always shows Jesus on the cross and includes an array of other details. In this genre of literature, however, the focus is on the magical powers of the cross itself. Thus, the cross stands without the figure of Christ, each arm identified by a name. The *haräg* around the illumination and at the top of f. 1r is the distinctive one employed in certain magic scrolls, built on the visual theme of the watching eye.

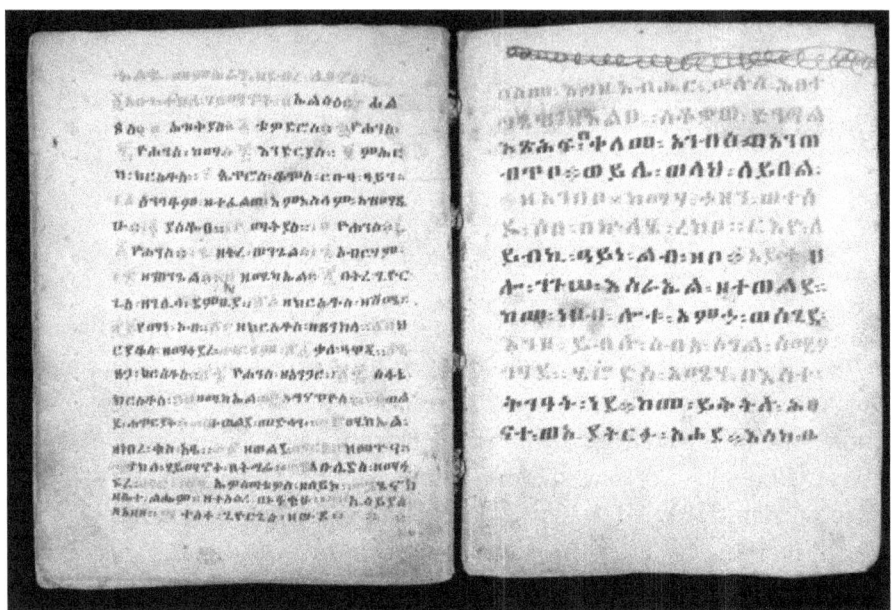

Plate 6: EMIP 6 (Marwick Codex 2), ff. 20v–21r

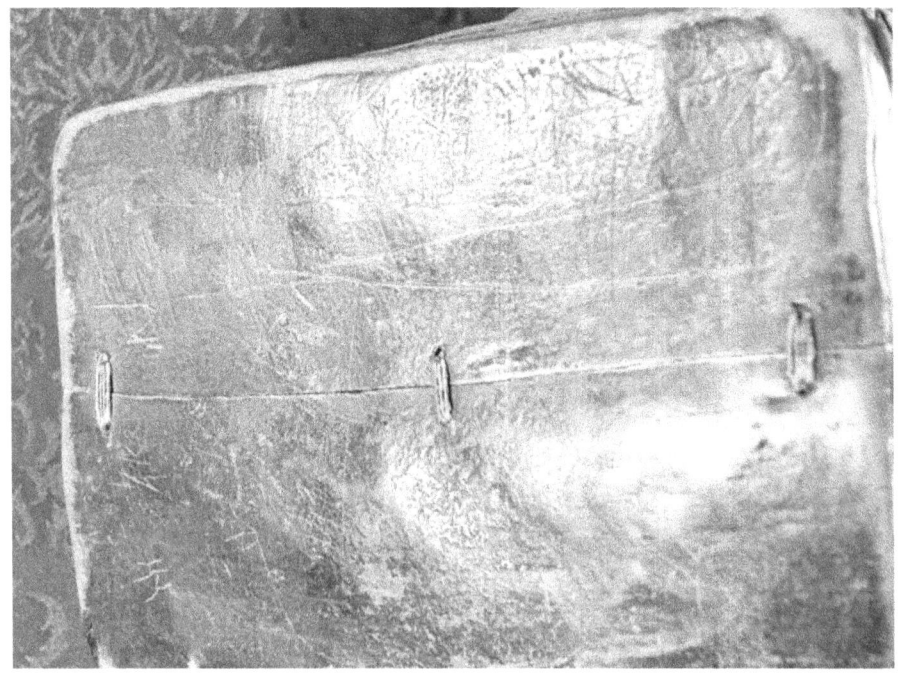

Plate 7: EMIP 7 (Marwick Codex 3), front cover

Plate 6: EMIP 6—Marwick Codex 2

This codex was copied in the 18th century and contains a collection of works, the longest of which has to do with the Christological controversies of the Gondorite era (ff. 6r–20r). This images shows the list (left, f. 20v) of the first forty abbots of Däbrä Libanos, from *Abunä* Täklä Haymanot to Täsfa Giyorgis of Wəddo and the first folio of the next work in the codex, Lamentations of the Virgin (ff. 21r–34r). Folio 21r shows the scribal practice of writing several lines of the first folio of a new work in red ink.[3] Thus, we see lines 1, 2, 5, 6, 10 and 11 written in red. In this image we can also see clearly the attachment between the second and third quires of the codex; the chain stitches show at the gutter. A later hand has added a crude *ḥaräg* in blue ink at the top of the new work.

Plate 7: EMIP 7—Marwick Codex 3

This late 18th century manuscript contains two works on the trinity: Sword of the Trinity (ff. 1r–38v) and Image of the Trinity (ff. 33v–38v). This image shows several typical features of the covers of Ethiopian codices: the rough-hewn surface, the grain of the wood, which is almost always oriented top to bottom (though there are a few exceptions), the frequent breakage and repair of cover boards, and the wear around the edges.

---

[3] Regarding the uses of red ink, see *PPM*, p. 264.

Plate 8: EMIP 8 (Marwick Codex 4), inside front cover and folio 1r

Plate 8: EMIP 8—Marwick Codex 4

This 19th century manuscript contains the Antiphonary for the Fast of Lent, *Ṣoma Dəgg^{w}a* (ff. 1r–93v), complete with musical notation. This image shows (left) the inside of the front cover with a small rectangle (52–30 mm) carved out of the wood to hold a mirror (no longer present). The inclusion of mirrors in the construction of the book is a feature aimed at a specialized and elevated social niche. As far as we know, the function of the mirror is normal (i.e., not spiritual, *per se*), aimed at personal grooming. In a Psalter, it may indicate ownership by a woman of a higher social class. A specialized liturgical and musical manuscript like this one points to ownership by a *debtara* (a priest with special training as a cantor and scribe), who take great care that their *Ṭəmṭəm* (turban) is properly worn. In the center of the image we can see the repairs that have been made to the bridle attachment of the cover to the text block. And on the right we can see the first folio of the Antiphonary with *ḥaräg* at the top, lines in red ink (lines 1, 2, 7, and 8) to mark the first folio of a new work, and the supralinear musical notation.

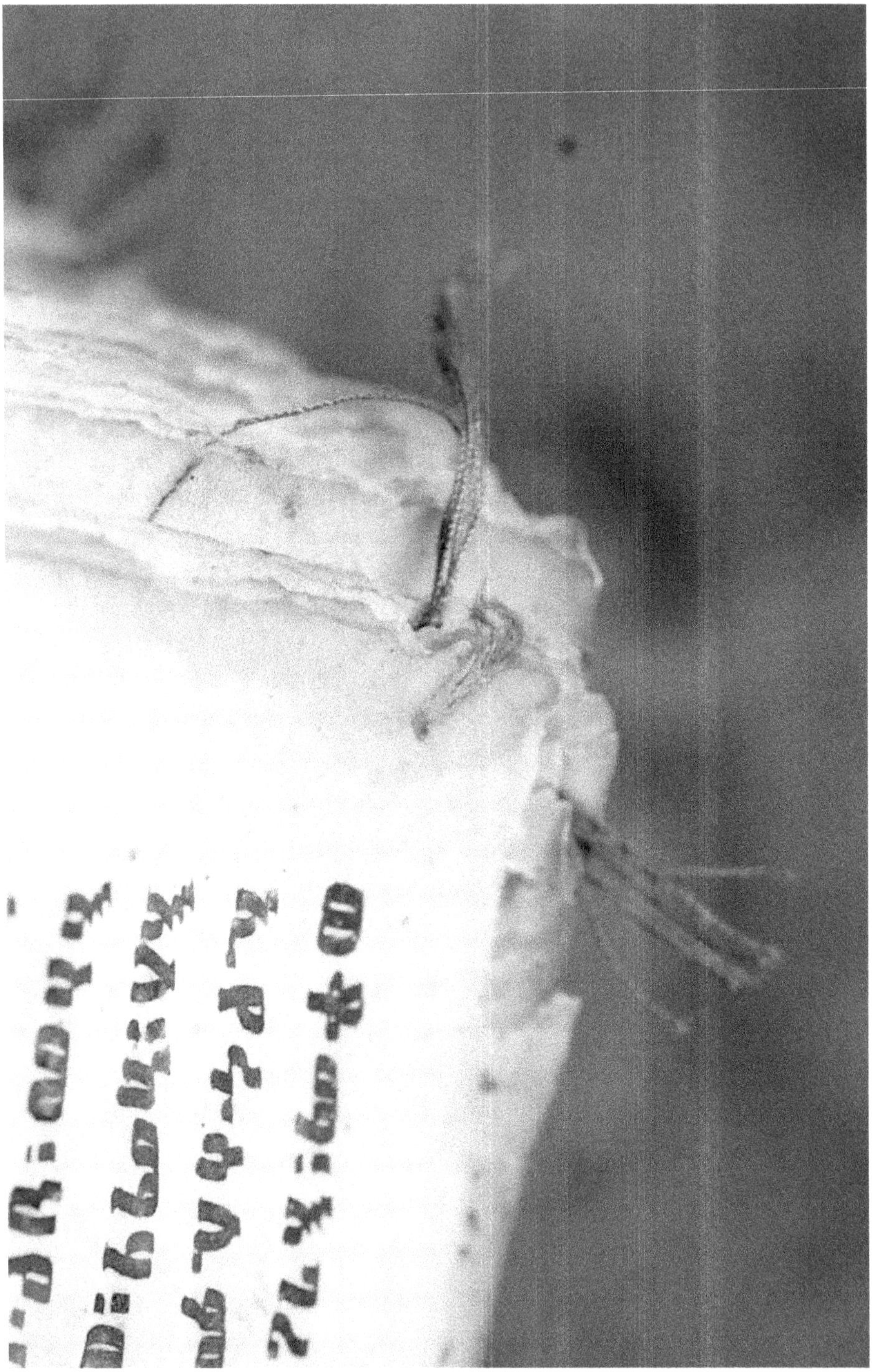

Plate 9: EMIP 9 (Marwick Codex 5), navigation strings in top fore edge

Plate 9: EMIP 9—Marwick Codex 5

Like many Ethiopian manuscripts that have been sold out of the country, this 18th century Psalter has been "retrofitted" with a collection of ten illuminations (ff. 5r, 20r, 37r, 58r, 76r, 95r, 117r, 136r, 151r, and 169r) to increase the value of the book. Each of the illumination in this book has been painted over the top of text by an artist that we have dubbed "the speckled garment artist" (examples of whose work will be shown below). We have digitized dozens of manuscripts that have been so "improved" by this artist. In many of these codices either the artist or the merchant has marked each of these illuminations with a piece of brown yard or thread sewn through the upper fore edge of the folios that contain paintings. The practice of sewing yarn or string into the fore edge of folios is quite old. Its original purpose was not to mark illuminations, but content divisions in the codex. This image shows the top fore edge of the codex. In the foreground we see part of the original navigation system of the codex: a piece of green thread sewn into the top fore edge of folio 120 to mark the section of ten psalms that begin at Psalm 121 at the bottom of f. 120r. The codex has several such old threads of various colors to mark sections within the codex. In the background we can see several examples of the brown string sewn in recently to mark the location of the images painted by the speckled garment artist.

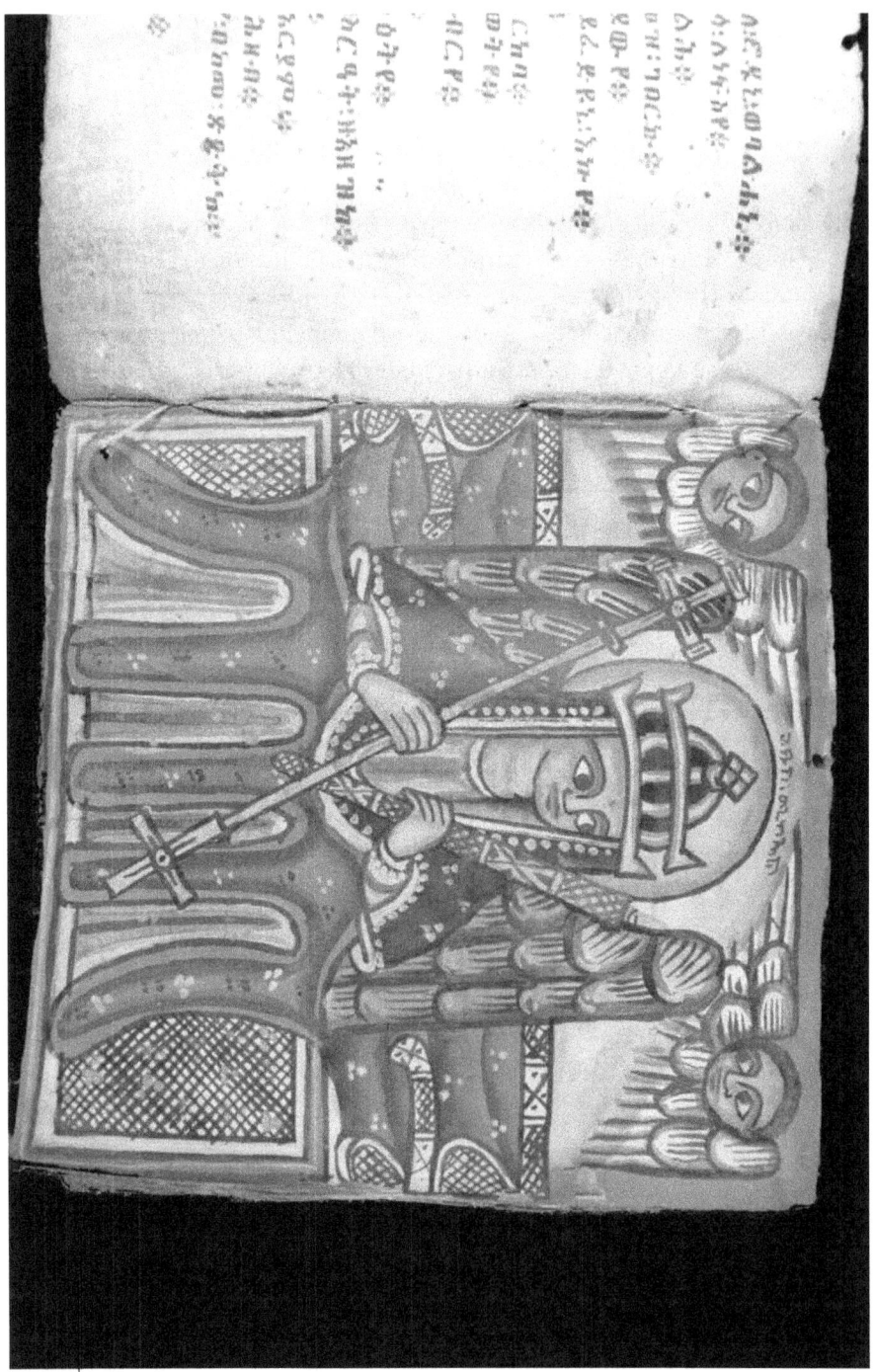

Plate 10: EMIP 9 (Marwick Codex 5), work of "the Speckled Garment artist"

Plate 10: EMIP 9—Marwick Codex 5

Folio 5r contains this illumination of the archangel Michael enthroned by "the speckled garment artist." It has been painted over the top of the text of Psalm 7:10–18. This artist proceeds by laying down a heavy layer of paint that covers the full page as opposed to the approach that employs the parchment as the background of the scene. This is necessary, of course, to cover the text.

Plate 11: EMIP 10 (Marwick Codex 6), tailband

Plate 11: EMIP 10—Marwick Codex 6

This image shows the base of this $19^{th}/20^{th}$ century Psalter between the inside cover and the text block. The focus is on the tail band, a small strip of leather braid woven of three strips. These are used only with books whose covers are leather bound, since the head and tail band are sewn onto the top and bottom of the spine of the leather covering. They serve as an anchor point into which the top and bottom of each quire is sewn. In these cases, then, the quire is anchored at top and bottom as well as in the four chain stitches that go through the gutter of the quire.

Plate 12: EMIP 11 (Marwick Codex 7), ff. 30v–31r

Plate 12: EMIP 11—Marwick Codex 7

This codex, completed on Ṭərr 21, 1915 of the Ethiopian calendar (E. C., which corresponds to January 29, 1923 in the Western calendar [folio 144r]) is comprised of 145 folios in thirteen quires. Quires one through seven are all made of five sheets. But quires eight and nine are made of seven sheets and quires ten through thirteen are made of six sheets. Scribes often number the quires as they are produced and before they are bound together so as to maintain their proper order.[4] There is some variation among scribes about the quantity and location of these quire numbers. The usual practice is a single number in the upper left corner of the first folio of a quire. The numbers are usually surrounded by a set of symbols akin to the full stop symbol, in red and black ink. This particular scribe has numbered each of the quires and done so in a manner that is a bit out of the ordinary. First, he has placed a quire number on both the first folio of the quire and on the last folio of the quire. Second, he has placed the number twice, once at the top of the folio and once at the bottom of the folio. This image shows the upper gutter between folios 30v and 31r, where we see not only the quire numbers for quires three (left) and four (right), but also a portion of the ḥaräg at the top of f. 31r which marks this section of ten Psalms.

---

[4] The reason for this becomes obvious when we realize how many months it may take to complete all the quires for one manuscript: three months for a Homiliary in Honor of the Monthly Feast of Saint Michael, five months for a Psalter and eight months for a Four Gospels manuscript (*PPM*, p. 266). Numbering the quires helps to maintain the order of the quires until they are all bound together at the end. Sergew (*BIE*, pp. 31-33) also discusses the length of time required to produce works.

Plate 13: EMIP 12 (Marwick Codex 8), f. 1r

Plate 13: EMIP 12—Marwick Codex 8

On paleographical and other grounds, this Psalter can be dated to the late 17th century. It provides a good example of the practice of arranging the material of a codex for various kinds of reading schedules. In fact, this codex contains two such systems. One set of notations has arranged the Psalms for readings on the days of the week. This image of the top of folio 1r shows the designation for Monday. The system for readings on the days of the week continues with Tuesday, f. 26v; Wednesday, f. 53r; Thursday, f. 77r; Friday, f. 108r; Saturday, f. 124v; and Sunday, f. 141r. The second set of notations designate readings for the church calendar: *Mäzagʷəʿ*, f. 3v; *Bərhan*, f. 39v; Paraclete, 46r; Winter [*Krämt*] and John the Baptist, f. 55r; Ascension, f. 57v; Lenten, f. 64r; Epiphany, f. 69v; *Nolawi*, f. 76r; Palm Sunday, f. 76r; *Qəddət*, f.89v; Flower [*Ṣəge*], f. 94v; Easter, f. 102r; Nativity, f. 107r; from *Səbkət* to *Astär'əyo* of Palm Sunday, f. 111r.). Based on this, Getatchew concludes that "the Psalter must have belonged to a church that used it during the liturgical calendar."

22 · *Ethiopian Scribal Practice 1*

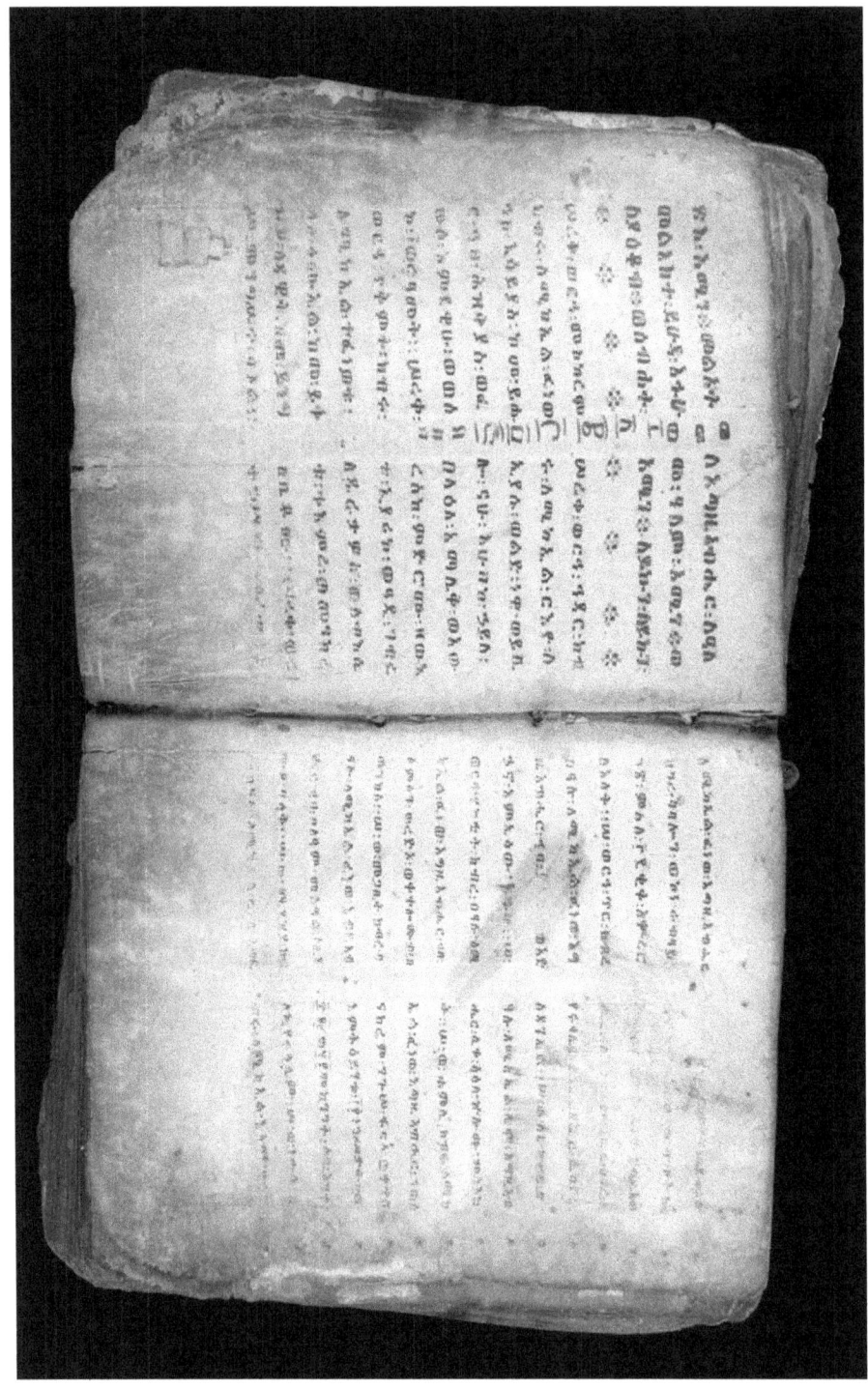

Plate 14: EMIP 13 (Marwick Codex 9), ff. 38v–39r

Plate 14: EMIP 13—Marwick Codex 9

The primary content of this early 18th century manuscript is the New Testament books of 1–2 Peter, 1–3 John, James, Jude and Revelation. These run from folio 1r to 79v. As with many, if not most, Ethiopic books, there are also a few smaller works included either in the end leaves or between the major works. Catalogued as "varia" and "notes," these small works can cover a variety of topics and are usually added by hands later than the original scribe. So, for instance, this manuscript includes an *asmat* prayer against thieves and robbers (in the front protection leaves), a list of rewards, in quantity of fruits, for praying certain prayers, like the Our Father, and for performing certain good deeds (f. 39v), a letter of greeting, in Amharic (also on f. 39v), and a record of the purchase of the manuscript on Mäggabit 2, 1940 EC (= March 11, 1948 AD,). This image shows folios 38v–39r which contains the other *varia* in this codex: a list of the Archangel Michael's twelve feast days of the year, with the reasons for their celebrations.

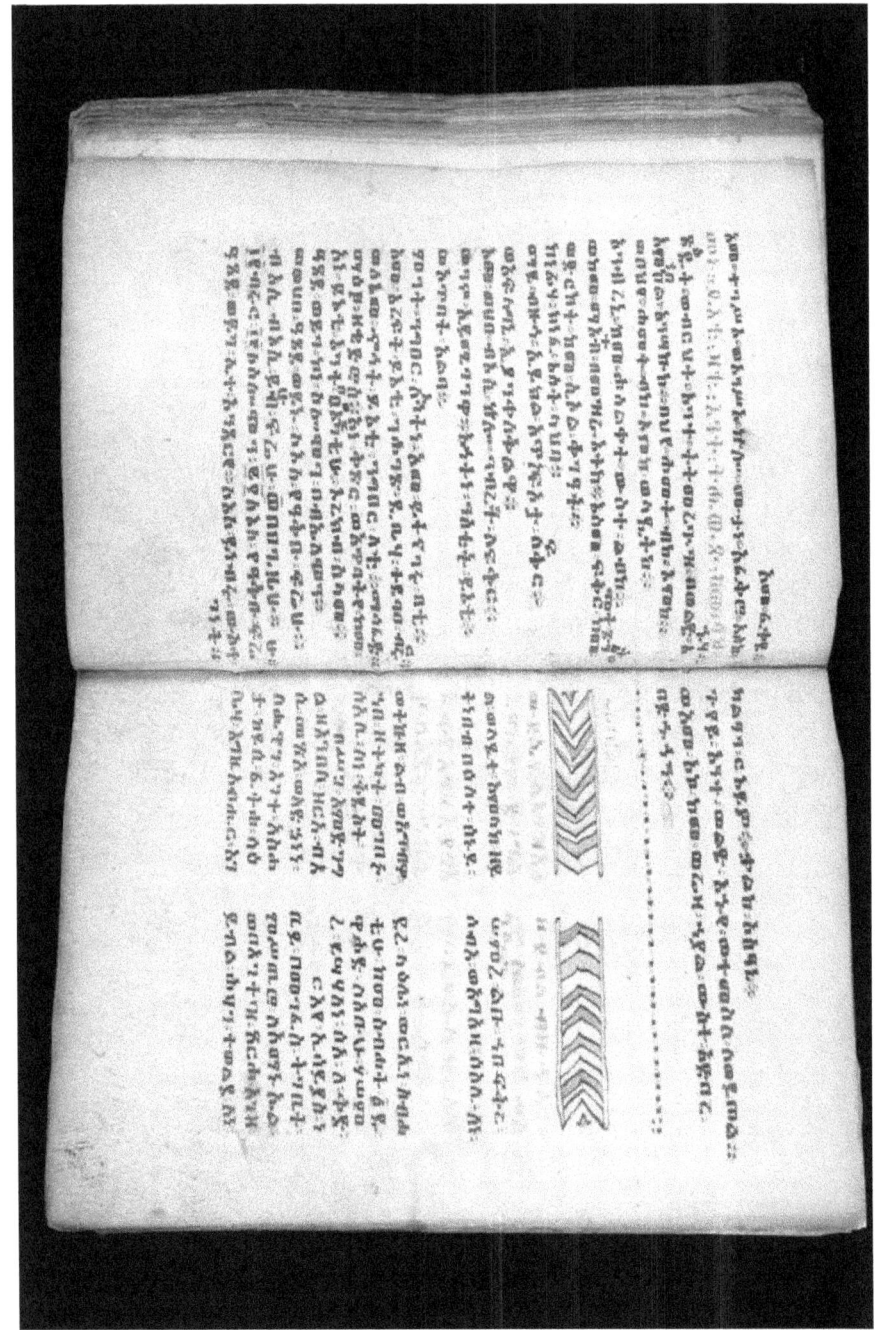

Plate 15: EMIP 14 (Marwick Codex 10), ff. 130v–131r

Plate 15: EMIP 14—Marwick Codex 10

Ethiopic Psalters not only have standard content (the 151 Psalms of David, the 15 Biblical Canticles, the Song of Songs, the Praises of Mary and the Gate of Light), the content is always laid out on the page in a standard way. The texts of the first three works are laid out in one column with each verse given its own line.[5] Thus, the left margin is justified; and the right margin is uneven and marked by a full-stop symbol at the end. The last two works in the Psalter are devoted to Mary and are always laid out in two columns,[6] both of which are evenly justified. This image shows the end of the book of Song of Songs (ff. 130v and the top four lines of f. 131r) and the beginning of the Praises of Mary. Three scribal devices have been used to indicate the break between works: 1) the line of alternating red and black dots; 2) a *haräg*; and 3) lines written fully in red ink (lines 1, 2, 5 and 6 of the new work).

---

[5] For a full description of practices related to laying out margins and columns on a fresh sheet of parchment, see *PPM*, p. 261.
[6] Having studied over 1,500 Psalters, I have encountered only two, both copied very badly, which lay the Praises of Mary out in one column.

26 · *Ethiopian Scribal Practice 1*

Plate 16: EMIP 15 (Marwick Codex 11), spine and back cover

Plate 16: EMIP 15—Marwick 11

The average external dimensions of Ethiopian Psalters change across time, from more or less square in the 16 and 17th centuries (this Psalter is dated to the late 16th century) to European-shaped books with an aspect ratio of 10:6 (height to width) by the 20th century. This image shows the spine of the book with its beautifully woven Coptic chain stitches attached with bridle attachments at four locations to the cover boards.[7] The holes in the quires at head and foot of the spine are for attaching the quires to a head band and tail band if the book were ever leather bound. The fact that these holes appear in virtually all quires (whether in leather bound or unbound books) would indicate that they are a standard part of the preparation of sheets into quires for books.

---

[7] For a discussion of the binding process, see *MP Bookmaking*, p. 16 as well as the picture on p. 2.

Plate 17: EMIP 16 (Marwick Codex 12), ff. 32v–33r

Plate 17: EMIP 16—Marwick 12

After Psalters and Gospels of John, the most common Ethiopic book is the Homiliary in Honor of the Monthly Feast of the Archangel Michael.[8] This work is arranged for the (thirteen) months of the Ethiopian calendar and provide materials for use in the celebrations for that month. The entry for each month is comprised of four elements: 1) a homily; 2) a miracle story involving the work of the Archangel Michael; 3) an entry from the Synaxary involving Michael; and 4) a concluding *sälam*, or greeting. This image shows an illumination of Saint Michael helping Samson to kill the Philistines with the jawbone of an ass (left, f. 32v), and the beginning of the entry for the month of Mäggabit (right, f. 33r). The word "Mäggabit" has been written in ink pen in the upper margin and we also see the lines of text written entirely in red ink (lines 1, 2, 6, 7, 11 and 12). This is one of a minority of manuscripts where the illuminations seem to be original to the codex, i.e., painted around the time it was copied.[9]

---

[8] Sergew (*BIE*, p. 34) lists as the most common in the ecclesiastical sphere as Psalters, Miracles of Virgin Mary, Miracles of Jesus, Missal, Funeral Ritual and the Book of Baptism. In the private sphere he lists the most common as the Gospel of John, Sword of the Trinity, Acts of Täklä Haymanot, Acts of Gäbrä Mänfäs Qəddus and the Psalter.

[9] Sergew (*BIE*, pp. 29-30) describes the course of instruction for students to become painters.

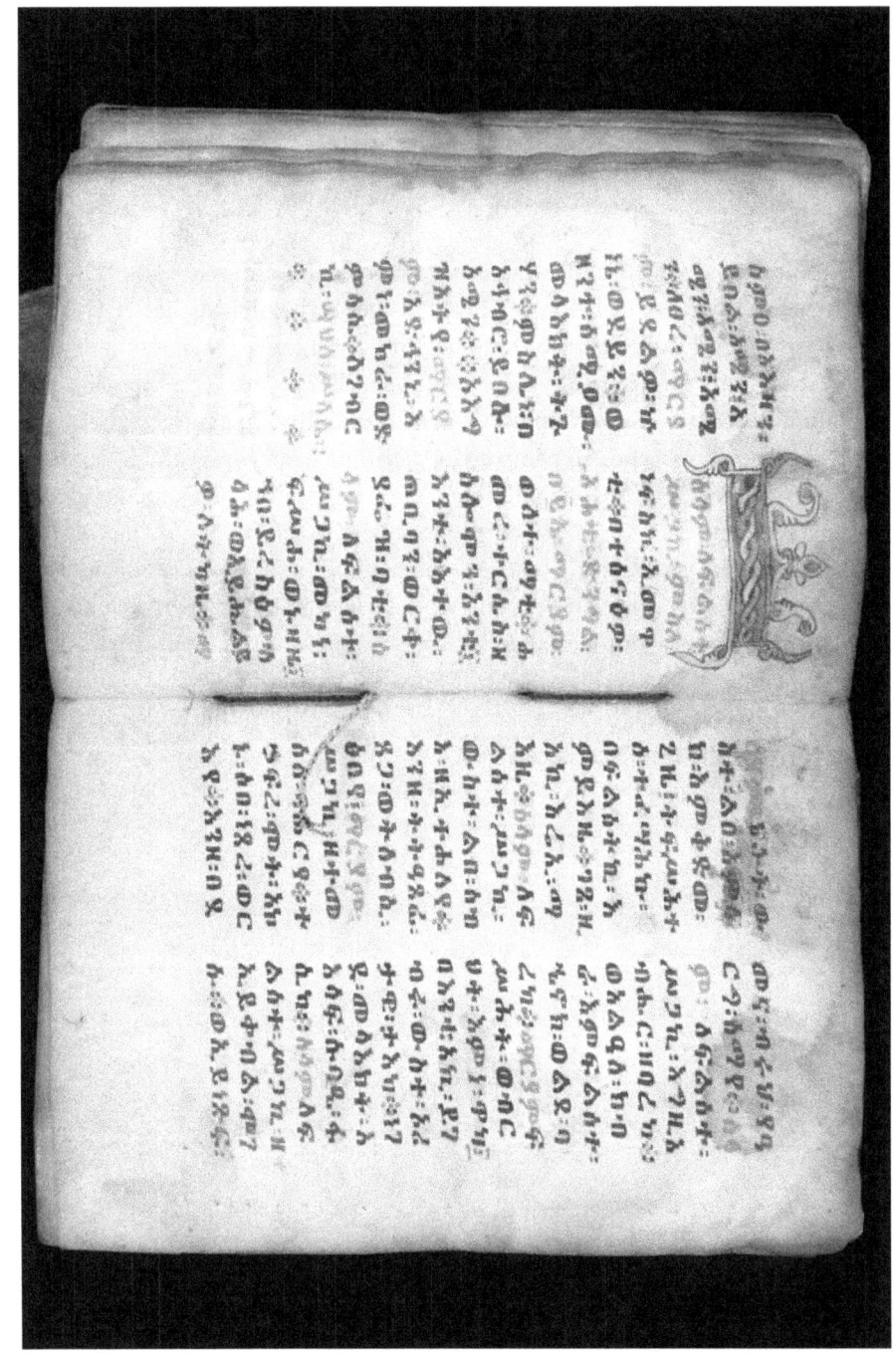

Plate 18: EMIP 17 (Marwick Codex 13), ff. 35v–36r

Plate 18: EMIP 17—Marwick 13

This (early) 20th century manuscript contains a collection of mostly short works all of which have one thing in common: they rhyme. The genre known as the "Image," has a series of stanzas which extol the physical features of the saint being described, often beginning from the top of their head and moving through every feature of their body down to their feet—thus, the name Image. But each stanza of an Image has five lines and each of the lines end in the same syllable or sound. This manuscript includes three such Images: Image of Mary's Assumption (ff. 35v–38v), Image of Jesus Christ (ff. 65v–71v), Image of the suffering of George (ff. 73v–82r). In addition, there are fully eleven other hymns, and greetings, most of which share this same characteristic of rhyme. The photograph here shows ff. 35v and 36r. Column one on folio 35v contains the conclusion of the Hymn to Mary "Rejoice Mary, the Pasch of Adam," a line of four full-stop symbols being used to designate the end of the work. At the head of column two is a beautiful *ḥarǟg*, which, along with the lines (1, 2, 5 and 6) written entirely in red ink, mark the beginning of the new work, Image of Mary's Assumption. Even without knowing the Gəʿəz alphabet, one can note that each stanza begins with the word ስላም written in red ink and that within each stanza, the last letter before every full-stop symbol (and half-stop symbol) is the same.

32 · *Ethiopian Scribal Practice 1*

Plate 19: EMIP 18 (Marwick Codex 14), f. 108r

Plate 20: EMIP 19 (Marwick Codex 15), spine

Plate 19: EMIP 18—Marwick Codex 14

Not infrequently, during the process of preparation, the parchment is torn and must be repaired.[10] If the parchment is sewn while it is still wet, then, when the entirety dries—sheet and stitches—the stitches will have shrunk and pulled the edges of the parchment together in such a way that the repair looks almost like a healed scar. This is in contrast to "dry repairs" of parchment that is torn after the book is finished and in use. This image shows a wet repair of unusual length. The use of repaired parchment is frequent among manuscripts from so-called "common" sociological niches.

Plate 20: EMIP 19—Marwick Codex 15

This manuscript of Praises of God was copied in the late 17th century and has undergone much use. More often than not, a common book of this age will have worn out the binding to the extent that its chain stitching must be repaired or replaced. In the case of this manuscript, a portion of the original stitching is still in place. But a series of repairs has been effected, seemingly to hold the manuscript together until a full repair could be effected.

---

[10] For a complete description of the parchment-making process, see *PPM*, pp. 255ff; *BIE*, pp. 9ff; *MP Bookmaking*, pp. 7-10; and the videocassette, *The Parchment Makers: An Ancient Art in Present-Day Ethiopia* (Sola Scriptura, 2000), available from Hope College.

Plate 21: EMIP 20 (Marwick Codex 16), ff. 136v–137r

Plate 21: EMIP 20—Marwick Codex 16

Manuscripts are datable by various means. The most fortunate case for the cataloguer would be where a full colophon specifies scribe, client, location and date of copying. This virtually never happens with Ethiopic manuscripts. The least fortunate case would be where there is no internal information in the manuscript at all with which to provide such answers. In these cases, the cataloguer is left to their knowledge of the development of Ethiopic letters across time (paleography). Because of the highly conservative character of the Ethiopian scribal tradition, this is a difficult judgment to make, even for the experienced eye. This particular manuscript of Images provides us with a scenario somewhere between these two extremes. The codex mentions in passing (on folio 137r, line 2, with black and red lines above and below) the name of the then-current king, Iyyo'as, whom we know reigned from 1747–1761 A.D.

Plate 22: EMIIP 21 (Marwick Codex 17), front cover and f. 1r

Plate 22: EMIP 21—Marwick Codex 17

The front and back cover boards on this early 19th century copy of Praises of Mary have been broken and repaired in the same way. The outer parts of the cover boards were apparently lost and replacement boards were found and sewn with string onto the small portion of the board that remained. Interestingly, the grain of the replacement board is horizontal, rather than the usual vertical and in contrast to the portion of the original board that remains. Folio 1r shows several interesting scribal features: a *ḥaräg* of geometric shapes (rather than the more usual interwoven, vine-shaped tendrils), lines in red ink (lines 1, 2, 5, 6, 9 and 10) to indicate a new work and interlinear musical notation. The latter continues only for the portion of Praises of Mary devoted to Monday (ff. 1r–2v).

Plate 23: EMIP 22 (Marwick Codex 18), top of the spine

Plate 24: EMIP 23 (Marwick Codex 19), front cover and three-quarter binding

Plate 23: EMIP 22—Marwick Codex 18

This image shows the top of the spine of this 20th century Psalter. From this angle (and since the codex has not been leather bound), we can see how it is that the quire comprises the basic building block of codex construction.[11] The book is made of fourteen full quires and one protection sheet at the front (visible on the far right of this image). The quires are comprised of from three to five sheets.

Plate 24: EMIP 23—Marwick Codex 19

One characteristic of the more deluxe manuscript is leather binding of the spine and covers. If the book is leather bound, it is usually a full binding, coving the spine and all of the boards. This 19th century Gospel of John, however, is three-quarter bound. The leather binding provides an opportunity to include head and tail bands and to stitch the top and bottom of each quire to the head and tail bands. These are sewn, in turn, to the spine of the leather binding. In the case of this manuscript, though, there is no head or tail band, but the quires are sewn directly to the leather binding.

---

[11] For a description of the construction of a quire by scribes, including the practice of laying sheets flesh side to flesh side and hair side to hair side, see *PPM*, p. 262.

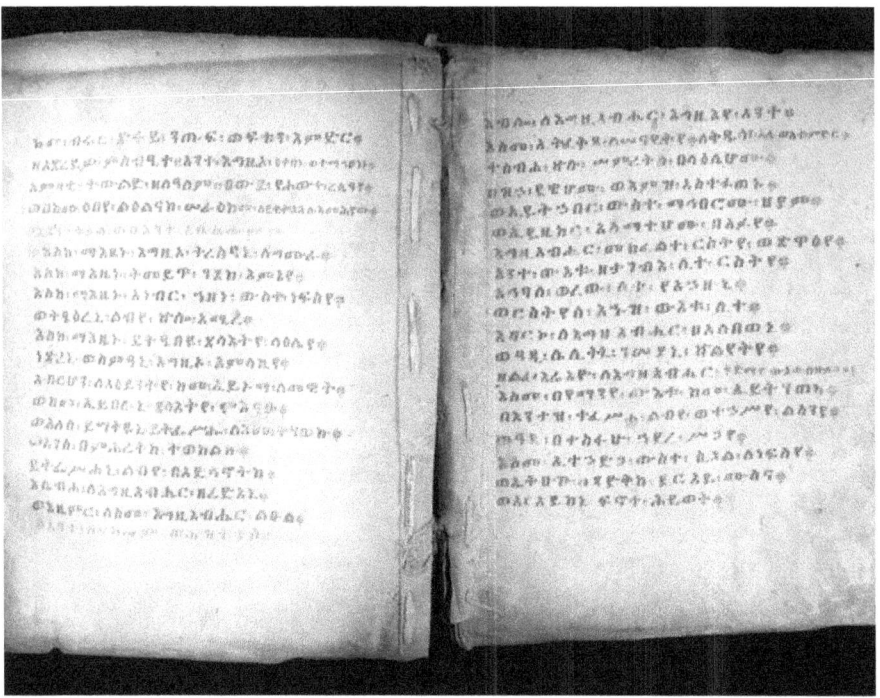

Plate 25: EMIP 24 (Marwick Codex 24), ff. 8v–9r, gutter

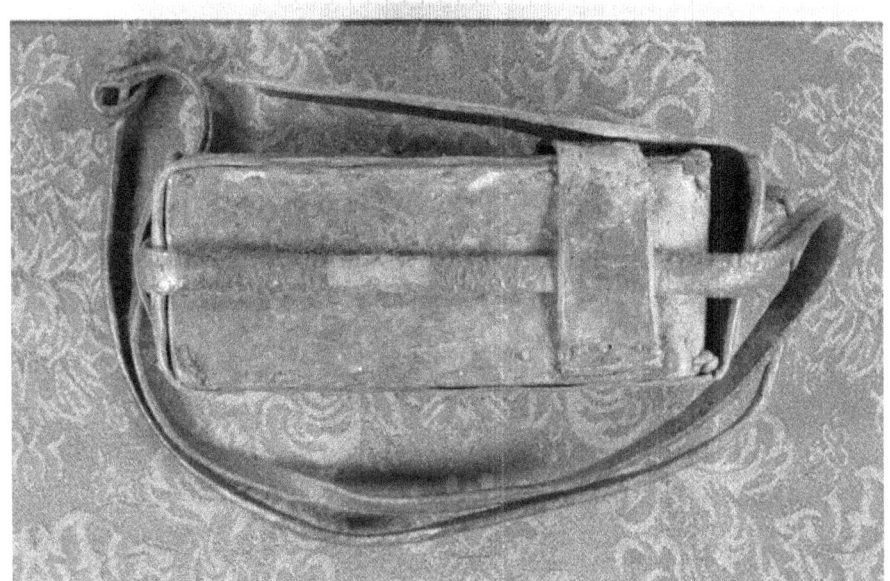

Plate 26: EMIP 25 (Eliza Codex 4), side view of *maḥdar*

Plate 25: EMIP 24—Marwick Codex 20

Occasionally, books become so worn that not only the binding along the spine is destroyed, but the outer sheet of each quire begins to wear through on the back (spine) edge. At this point, the book begins literally to fall apart. One form of repair is to fold small strips of parchment around the outside of the quire. This image shows folios 8v and 9r, where just such a repair has been made to the first and second quires of this early 18th century Psalter.).

Plate 26: EMIP 25—Eliza Codex 4

Plate 1 shows an example of a double slip case (*maḥdar*) with strap. This photograph shows the other common form that they take: a single container with a fold-over flap to protect the book (in this case a 20th century book of *Images*) from the elements.

Plate 27: EMIP 26 (Eliza Codex 5), ff. 84v–85r

Plate 27: EMIP 26—Eliza Codex 5

This 20th century codex contains the Anaphora of Our Lady (ff. 1r–29v) and Images of Mary (ff. 29v–47r, Jesus Christ (ff. 47r–63r) and Michael (63r–77r). Following these are fully 18 blank folios (77v–95v). Some have been prepared to receive text, others have not. This photograph shows a full sheet (ff. 84v–85r) at the center of a quire. It has been prepared to receive text with four vertical lines marking out fore edge margins and gutter and with twelve horizontal lines marking out the text blocks for the two folios. One can note the relationship between the placement of the lines and the prickings: in some cases quite precise (e.g., the upper prickings for the vertical fore edge lines) and in some cases quite imprecise (e.g., the prickings marking out the location of the gutter margins and many of the prickings for the lines of text). In this image one can also see a wet-stitch repair (left fore edge), the binding strings at the gutter, and a hole in the parchment (right fore edge)[12].

---

[12] At this stage in our photography we would routinely place a piece of light green paper behind holes in the parchment to block out any text on the following folio from being confused with text on the folio in the foreground, a practice we later abandoned as unnecessary.

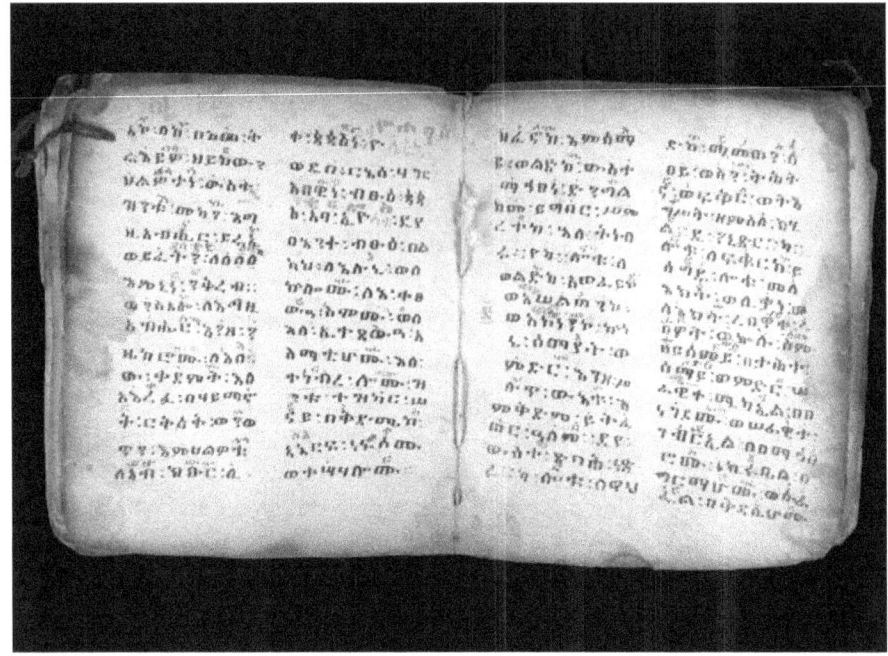

Plate 28: EMIP 27 (Eliza Codex 6), ff. 110v–111r

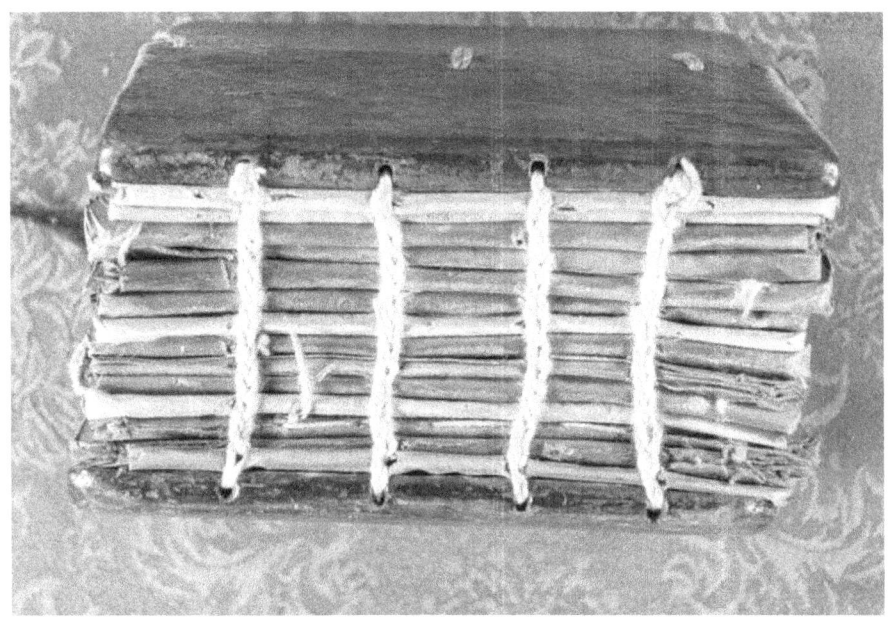

Plate 29: EMIP 27 (Eliza Codex 6), spine

Plate 28: EMIP 27—Eliza Codex 6

Missals can almost always be dated fairly precisely. This is because it is customary at certain points in the liturgy to mention the name of the then-current leaders of the church. In this case the Metropolitan Yosab (1770–1803) is mentioned on folio 110v (column 2, line 4). This image also shows several other scribal and codicological features: binding strings at the center of a quire, two sets of navigation strings in the upper fore edges of the folios (one original to mark content, another late to mark the location of recently painted illuminations), and interlinear musical notation.

Plate 29: EMIP 27—Eliza Codex 6

The binding and spine of this 18th century manuscript (see plate 28) has worn out and been repaired. In this image we can see that each of the quires has been fitted with a reinforcement strip (see plate 25) and that the codex has been rebound with new chain stitches.

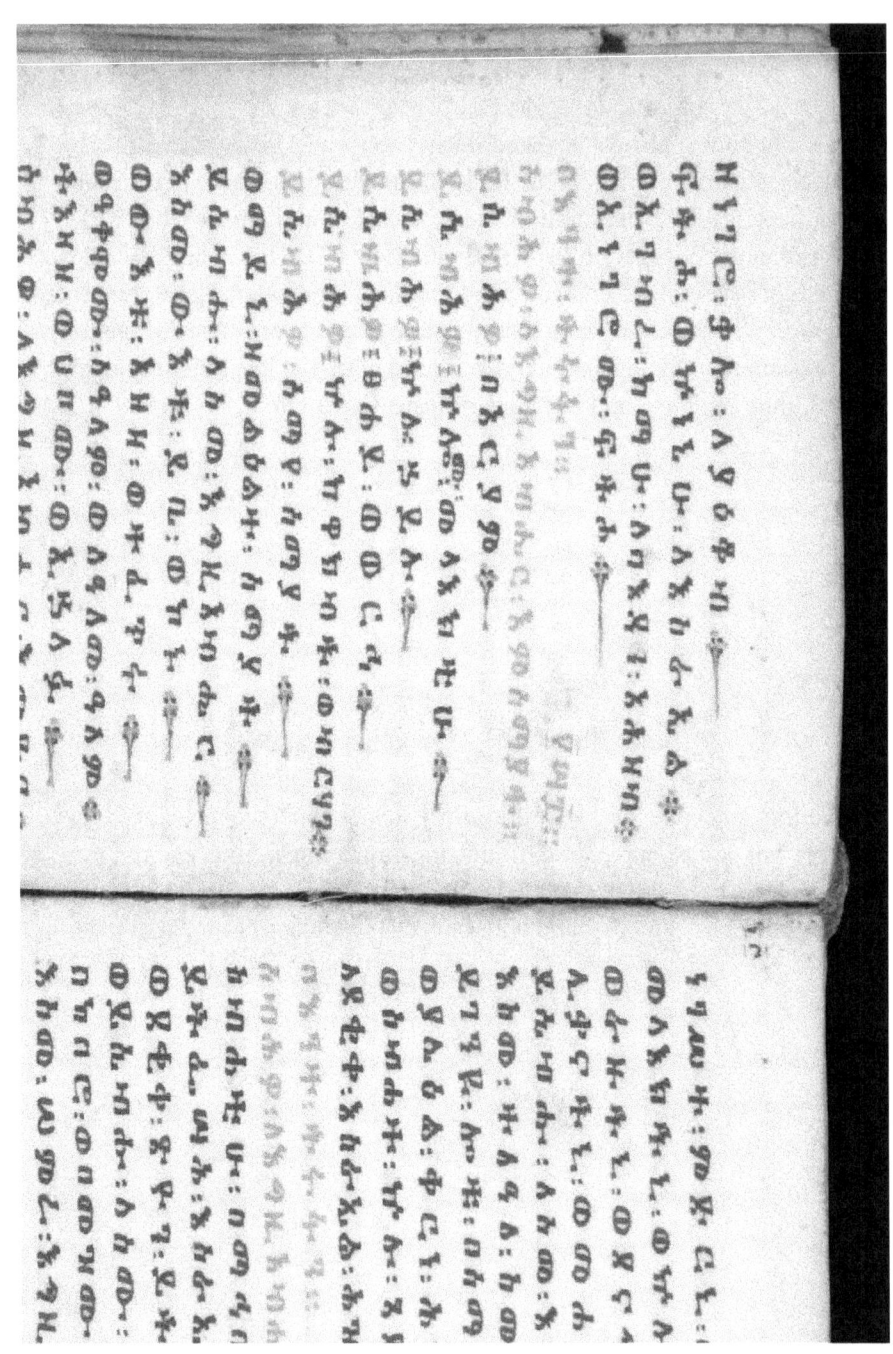

Plate 30: EMIP 28 (Eliza Codex 7), f. 106v

Plate 30: EMIP 28—Eliza Codex 7

We use the term "columetric layout of text" to describe the cases where scribes line up identical words in successive lines and accentuate their visibility by alternating letters in black and red ink. This columetric layout of text is very common among scribes for Psalm 150 and for the tenth biblical canticle (as we will show below). This manuscript is distinctive because it has several examples of columetric layout of text beyond the normal places. This image shows the text of Psalm 148. This scribe has accentuated the visibility of the word which appears at the beginning of five successive lines. This scribe does the same thing with texts in the fourth biblical canticle (f. 112v) in addition to the usual texts in Psalm 150 (f. 107v) and the tenth biblical canticle (ff. 116rv). In this image we can also note the distinctive form of the full-stop symbol (with lines extending from the right of the symbol and intersecting at some distance from the body) which flourished in the late 19th and early 20th century. This Psalter was copied in the late 19th century and sold again in 1899 E.C. (= 1906/7 A.D.; see the record of purchase of the manuscript on f. i v[erso]).

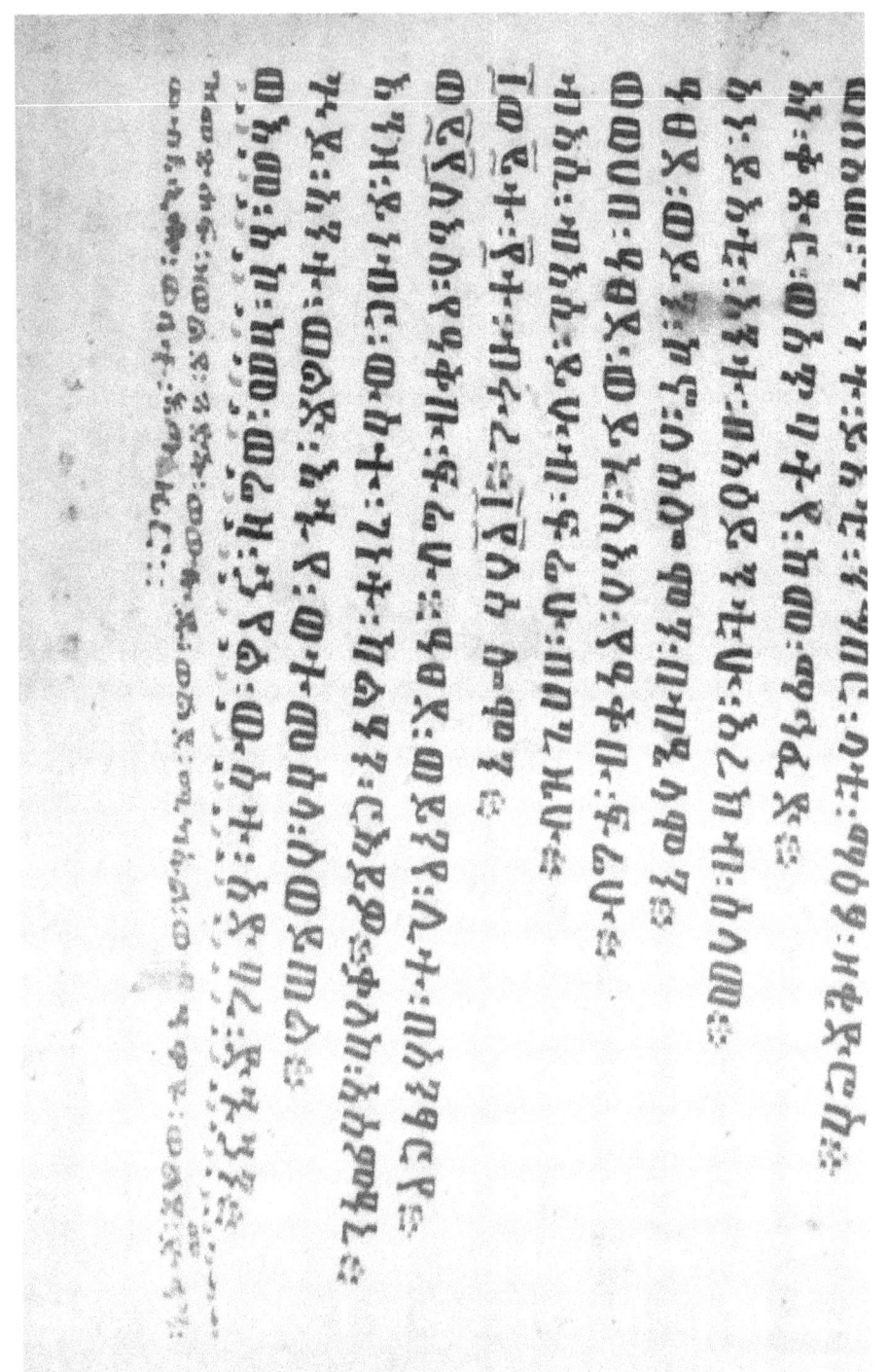

Plate 31: EMIP 29 (Whisnant Codex 1), f. 134r

Plate 31: EMIP 29—Whisnant Codex 1

It is not uncommon to find several notes of ownership in a codex as successive owners identify their claim of the manuscript. These can be located almost anywhere, in front and back leaves, and in margins. In Psalters, they are commonly located between Psalms and the Biblical Canticles, or between the Biblical Canticles and the Song of Songs, or between the Song of Songs and the Praises of Mary. This image shows the note of ownership by Wäldä Ṣadəq and his wife Wälätta Ǝgzi'bḥer on f. 134r, at the end of the Song of Songs. The line of alternating black and red dots is a standard section divider. During certain stages of the scribal tradition, the dots look more like semi circles, as in this 18th century codex.

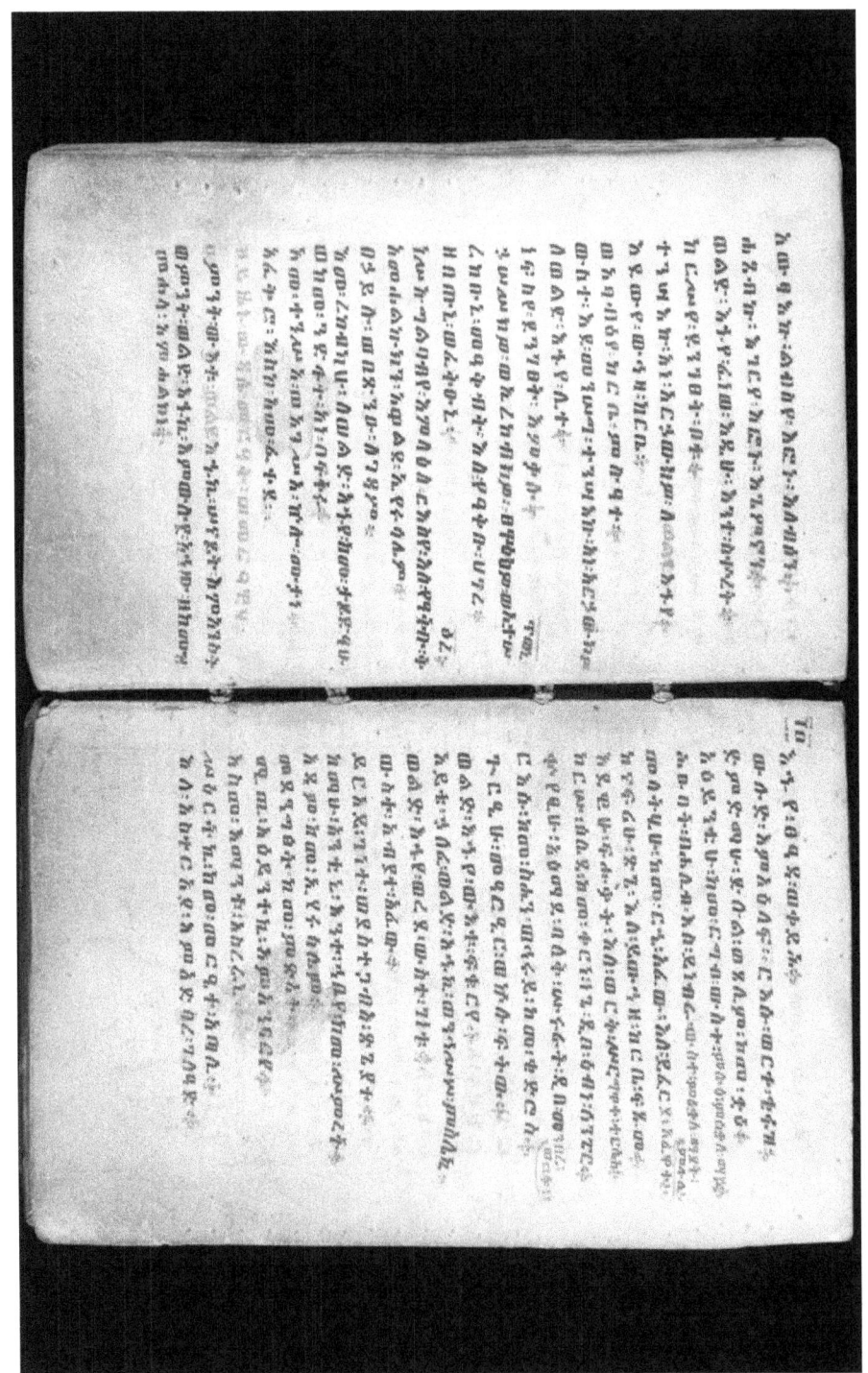

Plate 32: EMIP 30 (Whisnant Codex 2), f. 135v–136r

Plate 32: EMIP 30—Whisnant Codex 2

The first three works in the Ethiopic Psalter are always laid out in one column and with one verse per line. Each line ends with a full-stop symbol. This produces a text block that is justified on the right side and ragged or unjustified on the left. Scribes have always to contend with the issue of what to do when a verse of text is too long for a line. Whether or not this is even an issue has to do with the basic decision about the aspect ratio (height to width) of the folio dimensions and the size of the script. If a scribe employs a large script and the dimensions of the folio are tall and narrow, they will face problems at every turn. Most often the scribe makes a remarkably efficient decision that matches aspect ratio and script size to utilize most of the available space on the folio. But even with the best planning, there are always occasions where lines are too long for the space available. Scribes then have one of four options to choose from. The first has to do with whether or not to observe the right margin as laid out in the column scoring. If they have just a few too many letters, most scribes will write into the margin. Several examples of this can be seen on folio 135v where the scribe completes a line by writing into the margin and just leaves out a full-stop symbol. The second and third options for scribes are to place the extra text above or below the end of the line. When they do this, they usually mark the stray letters with black and red lines that partially surround the text. Examples of this can be seen on both folios. The final option for a scribe is to look ahead and see long lines coming and write some or all of the words on the line in a smaller script size. This option can be seen on folio 136r, lines 4, 6, and 8. The interesting thing about this scribe is that he employs all of these systems. In general, scribes prefer to complete the text above the line they are working on rather than below, unless there is no room above and there is room below. It is the rare Psalter, produced by the skillful scribe, that avoids ever having to put text on another line by varying the size of the script.

Plate 33: EMIP 31 (Earl Codex), inside front cover and f. 1r

Plate 34: EMIP 31 (Earl Codex), ff. 44v–45r

Plate 33: EMIP 31—The Earl Codex

Well over 95 percent of all Ethiopian books employ standard practice when it comes to wooden covers: the traditional heavy and tight-grained wood with the grain running top to bottom.[13] Consequently, it stands out when a manuscript has covers made of a light and wide-grained wood (as is the case with this 20th century manuscript containing three Miracles of Mary) or when the grain of the covers is horizontal to the orientation of the codex.

Plate 34: EMIP 31—The Earl Codex

Colophons with a date are rare, and welcome to the cataloguer. This image shows the folio (44v) where the scribe has written the precise date, Ṭǝqǝmt 27, 1933 EC, which equals November 5, 1940 AD. Ethiopic numbers are written with some form of black and red line written above and below them. The year 1933 is written in the first four characters of line three. In this image one can also see the penciled outline for a *haräg* at the top of folio 45r, marking the beginning of the Miracles of Mary.

---

[13] Sergew (BIE, pp. 24ff) describes the kinds of wood used on traditional book covers: *wanza* (Cordia Africana), Cedar and *wayra* (Olea Africana).

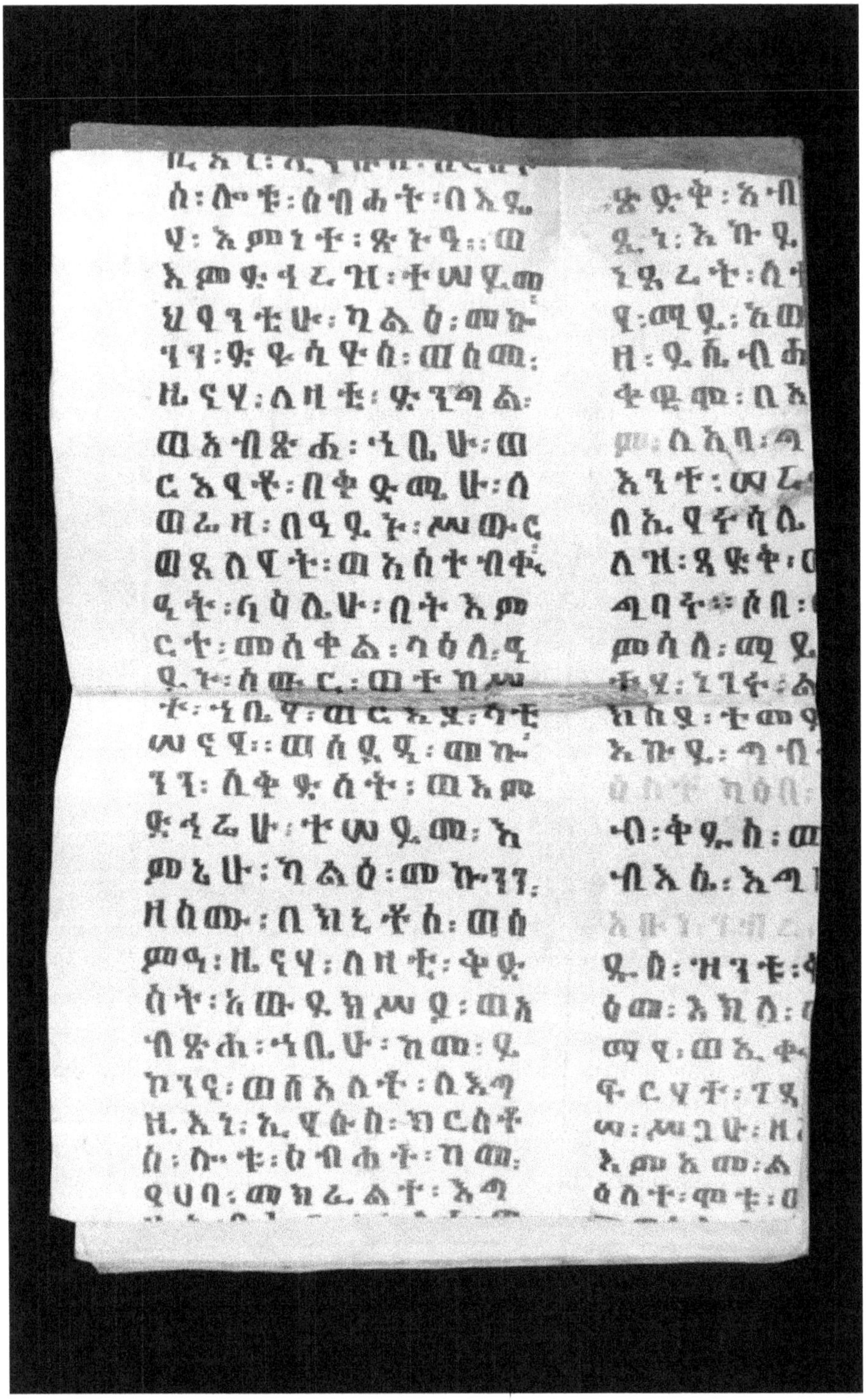

Plate 35: EMIP 32 (Delamarter Codex 1), ff. ii v(erso)–iii r(ecto)

Plate 35: EMIP 32—Delamarter Codex 1

Most scribes place a single protection sheet or a quire made of two or occasionally three sheets, between the front cover and the first folio of the first main work in the codex. We know that the scribes did not consider these folios as part of the content of the codex, because when they include quire numbers, they never include protection quires in the numbering of the quires. (This is the reason for the convention of numbering the folios in protection sheets with small roman numerals to distinguish them from the main body of the codex.) The sheets used for protection quires are characteristically of lower quality and value than the sheets that make up the rest of the codex. The scribe of this late 20th century baptismal ritual has made use of a rejected leaf from an older manuscript for one of the sheets of his protection quires. The rejected leaf comes from a Synaxary manuscript with the text for 5 Mäggabit: Eudoxia and Gäbrä Mänfäs Qəddus.

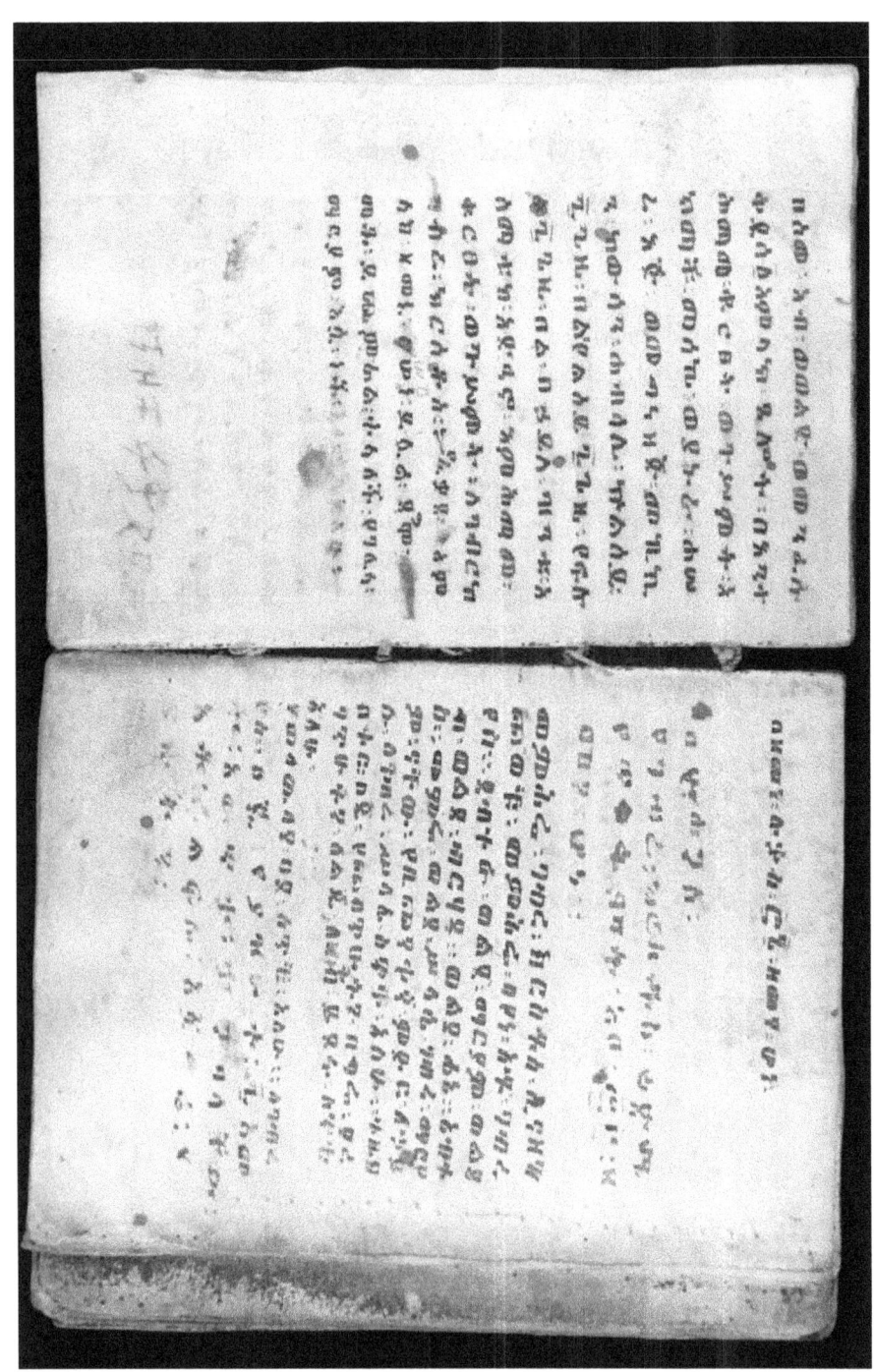

Plate 36: EMIP 33 (Eliza Codex 8), ff. 8v–9r

Plate 36: EMIP 33—Eliza Codex 8

Most of the manuscripts digitized by the Ethiopian Manuscript Imaging Project in North America have come from the social strata that would be labeled "common." The label is a bit of a misnomer in that the only people in the culture who could read and write Gəʻəz were trained priests, a relatively small percentage of the total population. But even granting that the manuscripts are much more "common" than those from elite ecclesial and royal sociological niches, there is still a great value to these manuscripts for the scholar. In the first place, they provide information about book culture in the common social classes. Most of the books that get preserved for libraries and museums are the uncommon books. And while these are very interesting and valuable in their own right, there has been a growing awareness about the importance of documenting the life of the ordinary people of the past and not just the social elites. Secondly, all manuscripts in Ethiopian culture are likely to contain not only copies of well-known works, but also unique, one-of-a-kind notes, records of transactions, wills, or military campaigns, etc. Throughout the life of the book these notes are added wherever there is space, often in the end leaves, but also in any other blank space in the codex. These spaces in manuscripts represent something like the national archives of Ethiopian culture. For instance, on f. 15r of this codex we learn that the book was originally copied by the scribe Gäbrä Maryam for one Gäbrä Krəstos. On f. 9v (plate 36) we learn that this Gäbrä Krəstos went by the title of *Mämhəre*, a title used for a priest, and that he was 73 years of age on the feast day of Abbo in the month of Ṭəqəmt (5 Ṭəqəmt). He even includes his will on this folio. On f. 117v, we learn that the book eventually belonged "to Gäbrä Ṣəyon whose teacher is Iyyo'ab; it was given to him by Lottu Səbḥat." On the same folio we read a prayer from one Wäldä Kahən, apparently sick at the time, who pleads that God may not separate him (by death) from the community. Through such texts we catch glimpses into the lives of common people in Ethiopia's history.

Plate 37: EMIP 34 (Eliza Codex 9), front cover

Plate 38: EMIP 35 (Eliza Codex 10), ff. 154v–155r

Plate 37: EMIP 34—Eliza Codex 9

When Ethiopic books are leather bound, they will very likely be tooled with standard patterns.[14] These include a cross on the front of the codex and a church on the back. This image shows the cover of this 18th century Psalms of David, shot with raking light to accentuate the tooling. The codex is one of very few that contains just the Psalms and not a full Psalter.

Plate 38: EMIP 35—Eliza Codex 10

In this image we can see several interesting features of this 19th century Psalter. The top ten lines of folio 154v mark the conclusion of Song of Songs, laid out in one column; folio 155r marks the beginning of Praises of Mary, laid out in two. An elaborate *haräg* and two lines of text written entirely in red ink stand at the head of Praises of Mary. A blank space would originally have dominated the lower half of folio 154v. A later hand has added a chant for Easter, with musical notation (the interlinear single characters).

---

[14] For a discussion of leather covering of wooden covers, see *BIE*, pp. 24-25. Sergew goes on to describe the various tools and patterns for tooling the leather.(pp. 25-26). Cf. also, *MP Bookmaking*, pp. 17-19.

Plate 39: EMIP 36 (Eliza Codex 11), spine

Plate 39: EMIP 36—Eliza Codex 11

This codex is an early 19th century book of Miracles, including five Miracles of Mary, three Miracles of Mercurius, two miracles of Abunä Täklä Haymanot, and ten Miracles of Jesus. One indication of the popularity of this genre of works is revealed in the wear patterns on this codex. The codex has been competently rebound with new strings in the same locations as the original strings. We can easily imagine that the original strings had disintegrated through wear and we can see the wear patterns on the backs of the quire folds, in some cases worn clear through. When the wear extends along the entire spine of a quire, the folios within simply come loose from the book and are easily dislocated and lost. At this point the only thing that can be done is to sew reinforcement strips around the quires and sew stab stitches through quire folios and the reinforcement strip to hold everything together. The repairs to this codex include a few small reinforcement strips.

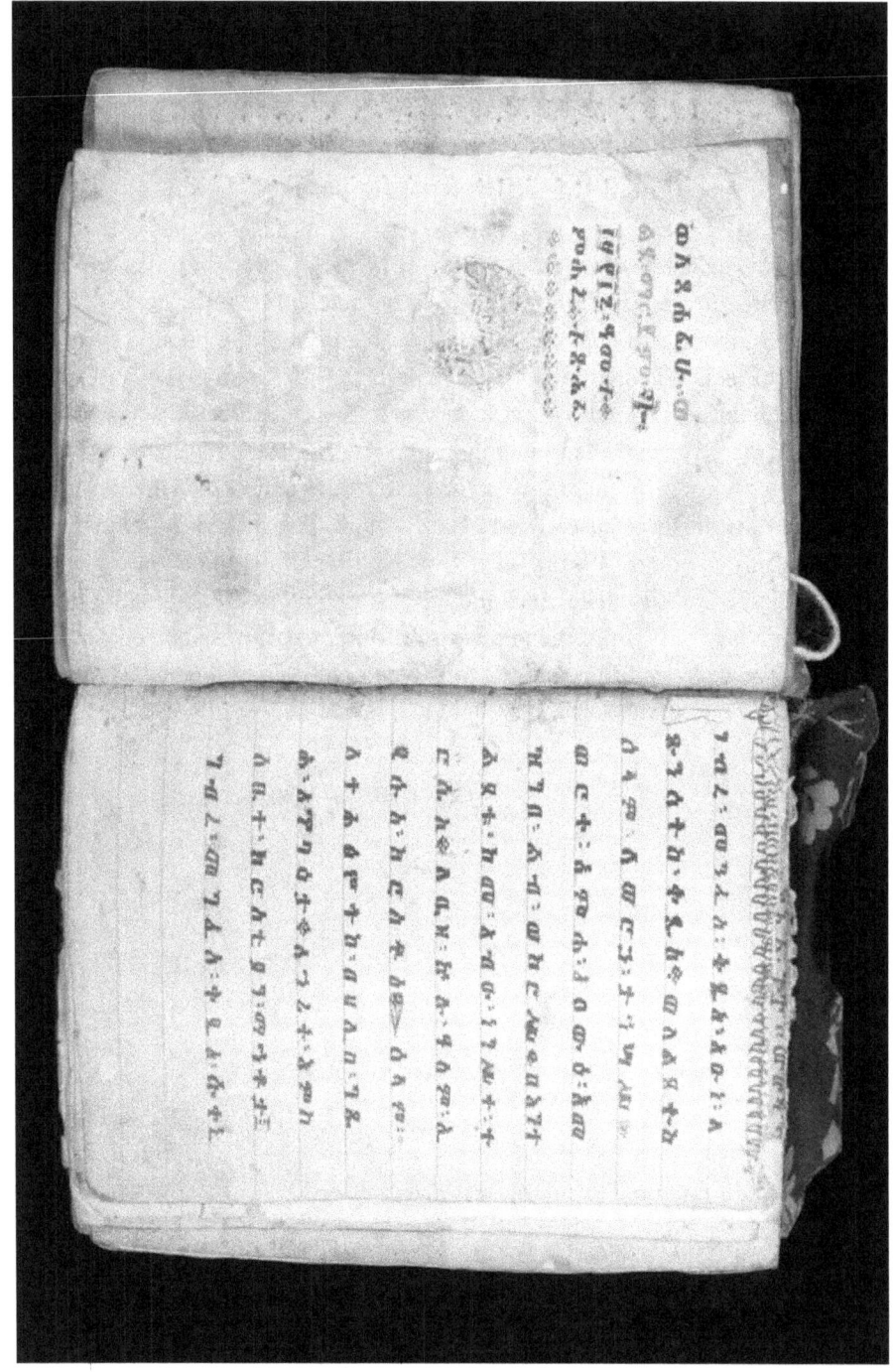

Plate 40: EMIP 37 (Eliza Codex 12), ff. 78v–79r

Plate 40: EMIP 37—Eliza Codex 12

This codex contains quite a number of rare features of Ethiopian book culture, including seals of ownership (ff. 16r and 78v), linen covers for the entire codex (this one came sheathed in two such covers), a host of Records and transactions and prayers (including a long letter written on a large piece of lined paper and tucked between the inner linen cover and the front board), a printed picture (of Italian origin) of Madonna and Child pasted onto folio 18v, a set of eight illuminations painted recently into the codex over the top of text, a quire with several sheets of lined paper, the inclusion of many sheets of parchment which have no writing on them and have not been prepared to receive text, etc. In addition, the codex contains quires from several different sources all joined into the one book. This particular image shows the join of quire 9 (left) and quire 10 (right). Quire 9 has several differences from the prior quires: 1)its measurements are irregular, apparently to trim it for inclusion in this codex: the height of the sheets is 138 mm; the width varies from 100 mm at the top to 93 mm at the bottom; the quality of the vellum is much finer and drier; 3) the side and bottom margins are mostly trimmed off; 4) there is no use of a full-stop symbol; 5) the hand is different; and 6) the folio stub visible between ff. 73 and 74 is cut very regularly (in contrast to the folio stubs visible in prior quires) about 7 mm from the gutter. Quire 10 has several sheets of lined paper.

Plate 41: EMIP 38 (Eliza Codex 13), linen cover and body of the codex

Plate 41: EMIP 38—Eliza Codex 13

Looks can be deceiving. This codex, containing the Gospel of John and Image of Raguel, is very recent. It was completed Ḥədar 23, 1993EC, or December 12, 2000. It is clearly dated by the main scribe's hand on folio 78r. It has no front cover board, but a linen cover has been placed around the manuscript in the traditional way.

66 · *Ethiopian Scribal Practice 1*

Plate 42: EMIP 39 (Eliza Codex 14), ff. 22v–23r

Plate 42: EMIP 39—Eliza Codex 14

The thematic repertoire of the "speckled garment artist"—at least as represented by the manuscripts that have come to us—is fairly limited. The image on f. 22v is of Saint George and the Dragon, which, after the Madonna and Child, is probably the single most-repeated illumination by this and other artists. Another ubiquitous image in Ethiopian iconography is that of the guardian angel with drawn sword and scabbard (f. 23r). This image is, in fact, the most frequent one placed by scribes and artists in magic scrolls; perhaps 85 percent of magic scrolls have such an image. Though this image is drawn very frequently by the speckled garment artist, in this 19th century book of Miscellaneous Prayers, the artist has labeled the angel as Kirubel (derived from the Hebrew word Cherubim), who is mentioned elsewhere much less frequently than any of the other angels, especially Michael and Gabriel, but even Rufael and Raguel. The usual pattern for the speckled garment artist is to paint eight illuminations in a manuscript. In most cases, the dealer marked the location of the illuminations with a string sewn through the fore edge of the folio. Based on the more than forty manuscripts that have come through the Ethiopian Manuscript Imaging Project that have been illuminated by this artist, the eight illuminations in each manuscript come from a pool of only about a dozen images overall.

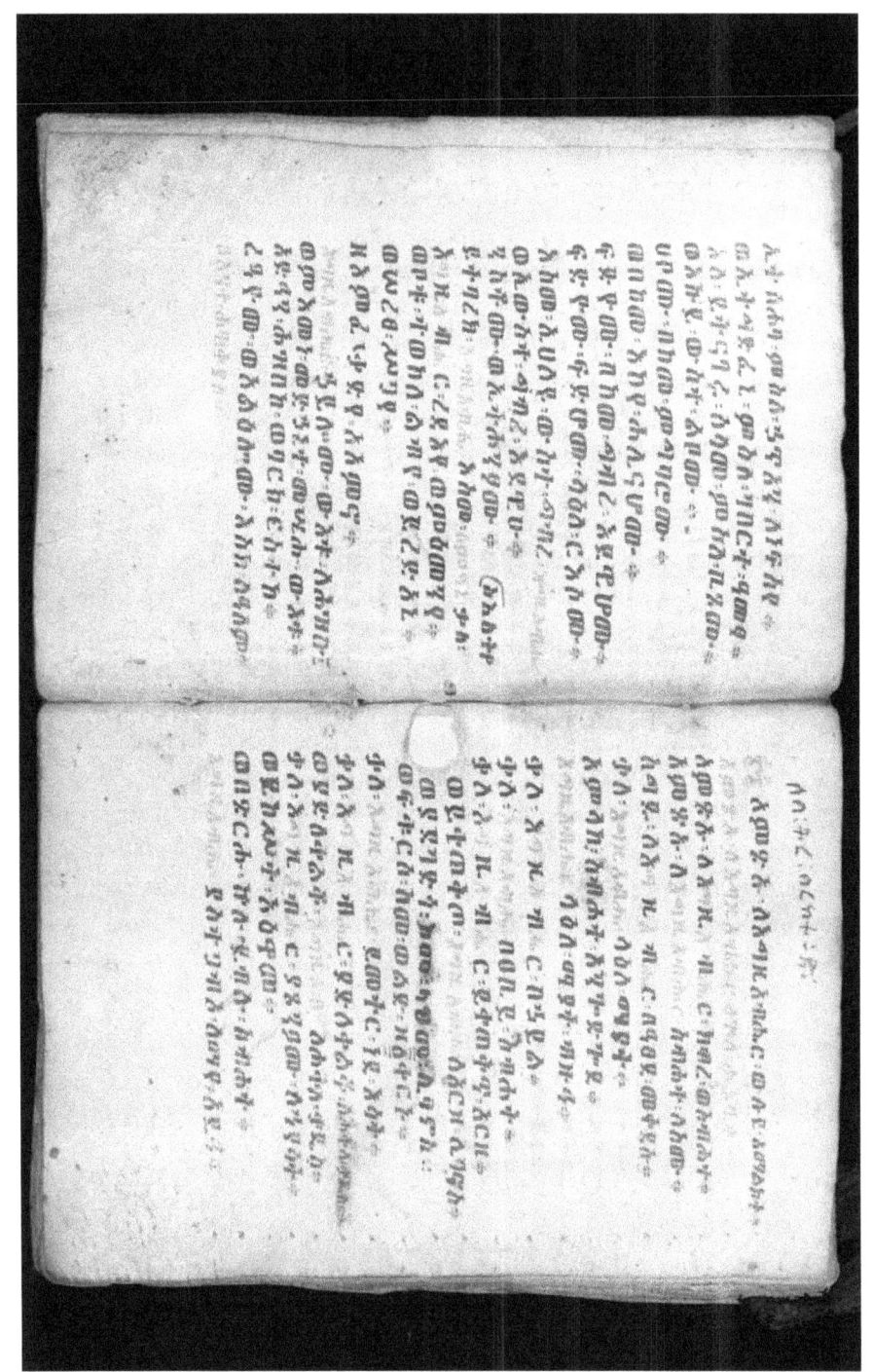

Plate 43: EMIP 40 (Eliza Codex 15), ff. 21v–22r

Plate 43: EMIP 40—Eliza Codex 15

In general, Ethiopian scribes usually use red ink to write the names of saints and members of the godhead.[15] When it comes to Psalters, though, we can observe a very interesting phenomenon. The two primary words that are candidates for writing in red ink are the word "God," እግዚአብሔር, which occurs all throughout the first three works in the Psalter (the 151 psalms, the 15 biblical canticles and the Song of Songs), and the name of Mary, ማርያም, which occurs throughout the latter two works (Praises of Mary and Gate of Light). In actual practice, all scribes use red ink for the name of Mary in the latter two books, but only some use red ink for the word "God" in the first three works. This 19th/20th century Psalter is one of the ones that gives red ink to both. One can see at least a dozen examples of እግዚአብሔር written in red ink on these two folios. In addition, this scribe does something only rarely done by other scribes and draws attention to the word for "God" by writing the letters in alternating red and black ink: on the left folio on line 13, and on the right folio on lines 3, 5, 9, 11, 16 and 18.

---

[15] For a discussion of the making of ink and various recipes for black, red and even gold ink, see *BIE*, pp. 14-17. Cp. *MP Bookmaking*, p. 12.

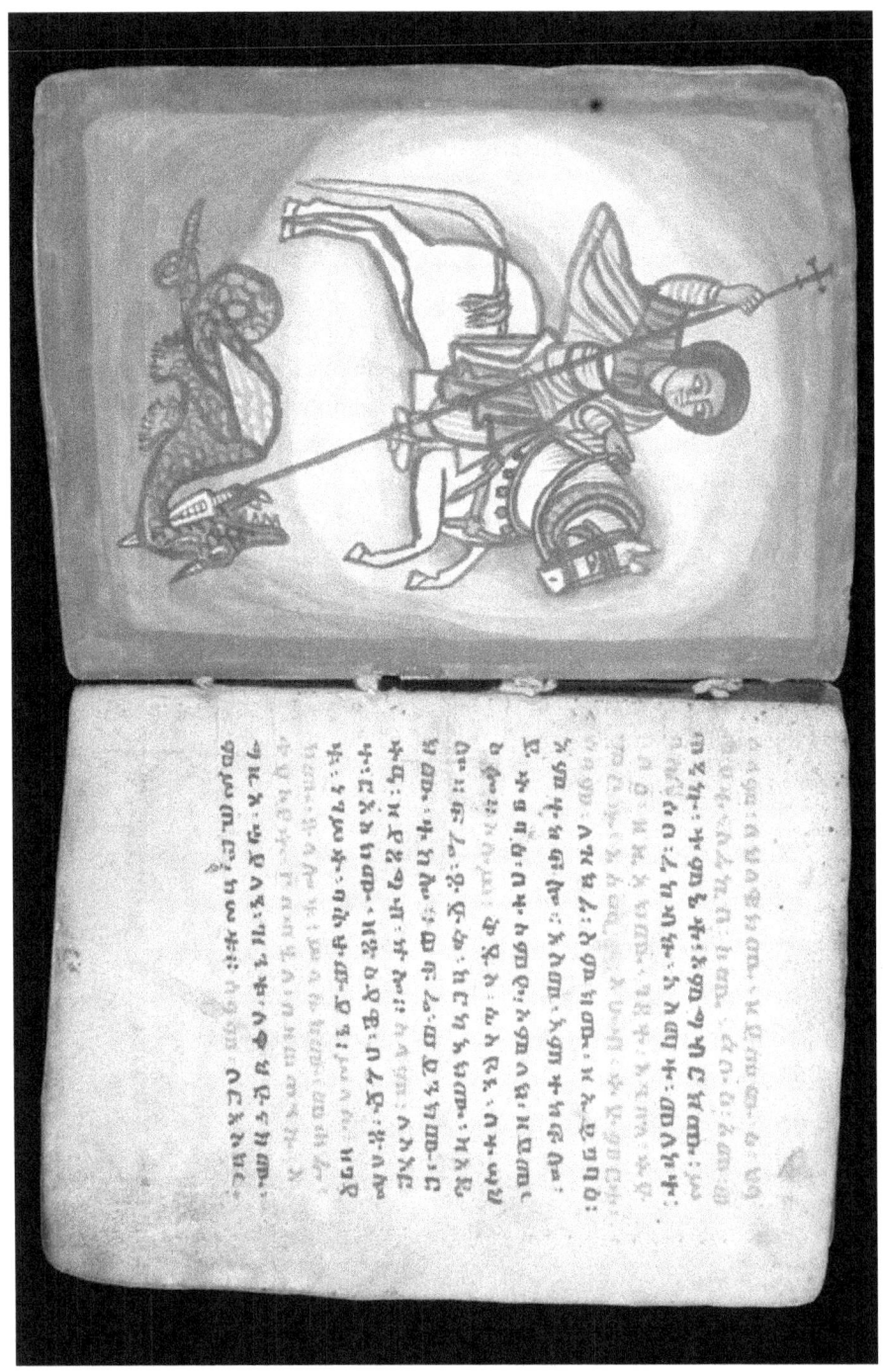

Plate 44: EMIP 41 (Eliza Codex 16), ff. 48v–49r

Plate 44: EMIP 41—Eliza Codex 16

This 20th century codex contains a collection of works on the Trinity. A hymn to the Trinity (ff. 7r–8r), the Story of the Trinity (ff. 9r–12r), Sword of the Trinity (ff. 12r–48r), and Image of the Trinity (ff. 49r–56r). The picture shows the first folio of Image of the Trinity (right, f. 49r, notice the lines of text written entirely in red ink) as well as an illumination of Saint George and the Dragon (left, f. 48v). This illumination and three others were painted over the top of text in the manuscript, presumably to increase its value for re-sale.

72 · *Ethiopian Scribal Practice 1*

Plate 45: EMIP 42 (Eliza Codex 17), spine

Plate 45: EMIP 42—Eliza Codex 17

The spine of this codex gives some hint of its age and the complex history of its production. In fact, the codex as it now stands is a composite of sheets and quires from at least seven different sources. At the beginning of the book are fragments from a Psalter (ff. 1, 2 and 20, quires 1 and 5). On these folios the text (of Biblical Canticles) is laid out in twelve lines per page. Second, is a fragment from a Gospel of John, including chapters 1:1–6:48 (ff. 3–17, quires 2 and 3). These folios are laid out in two columns and 16 lines per page. Third, is a fragment of the Computus, based on the year 7378 AM, or 1871 AD. These folios (18–19, quire 4) are laid out in 21, 19, 16 and 14 lines per folio. Fourth, is a fragment from another Gospel of John 20:2–21:17. These folios (21–26, quire 6) were copied in the 16th century and are laid out in two columns and 12 lines per folio. Fifth, is a quire with fragments from several works: excerpt from Image of the Icon (27r), Hymn to Mary (28rv), Image of Kiros (28v–29v), Asmat prayer against charm (31r–34r, quire 7) with folios laid out variously in 20, 23 and 24 lines per folio. This quire has been stitched together with a stitch running about 5mm from the gutter and attached to the codex secondarily with brown string. Sixth, is the largest fragment in the codex: Excerpts from the Horologium of Abba Giyorgis for the night hours (ff. 35–93, quires 8–13 and the first ten lines of quire 14. It is laid out in 12 lines per folio. Seventh, and finally, folios 93–98 (quire 14) contain *asmat* prayers against charms, It is laid out in 23 lines per folio.

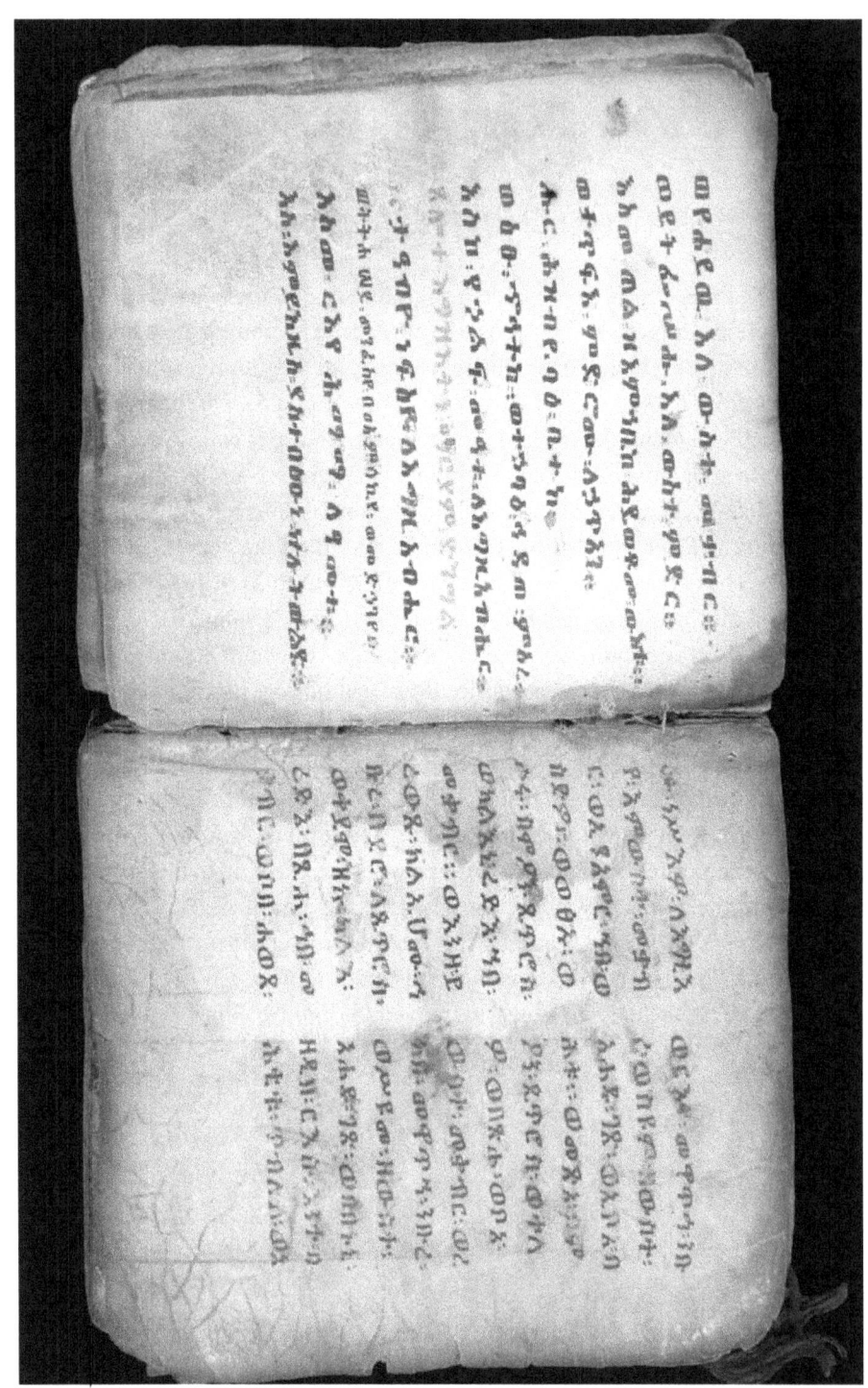

Plate 46: EMIP 42 (Eliza Codex 17), ff. 20v–21r

Plate 46: EMIP 42—Eliza Codex 17

This pictures shows the place where two quires meet. The folio on the left (f. 20v) contains the last part of the Song of Isaiah (part of the biblical canticles) in an 18th century hand; the folio on the right contains the Gospel of John 20:2ff in a 16th century hand.

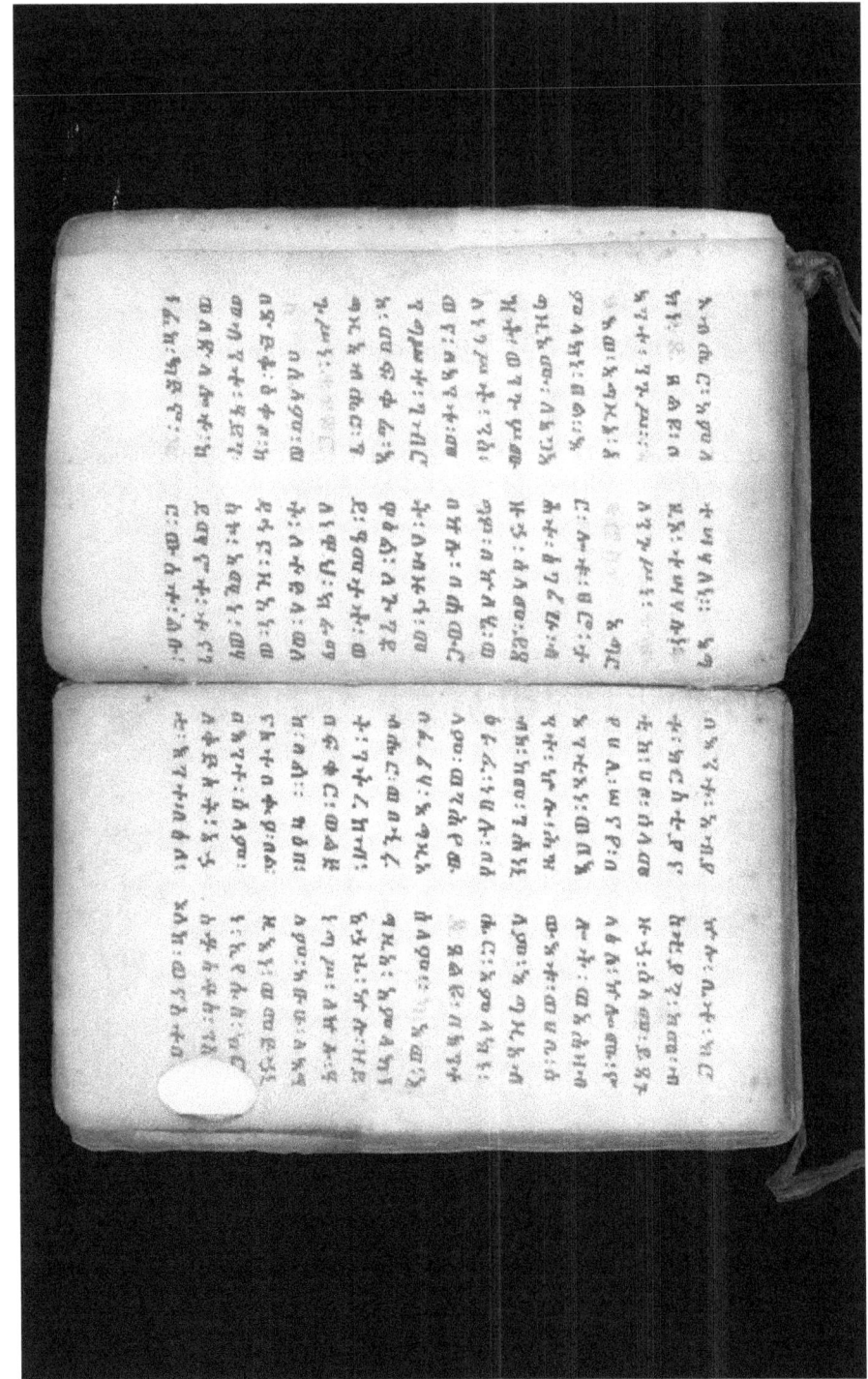

Plate 47: EMIP 43 (Eliza Codex 18), ff. 22v–23r

Plate 47: EMIP 43—Eliza Codex 18

Like the Missal, this book containing Office Prayers and Praises of Mary, mentions the name of the king at various places in the liturgy. On folio 22v (left), King Tewodros (1855–1868) is mentioned twice, once in column one, lines 13/14 and once in column two, lines 3/4. In both cases the name of the King, like the names of saints, is written in red ink.

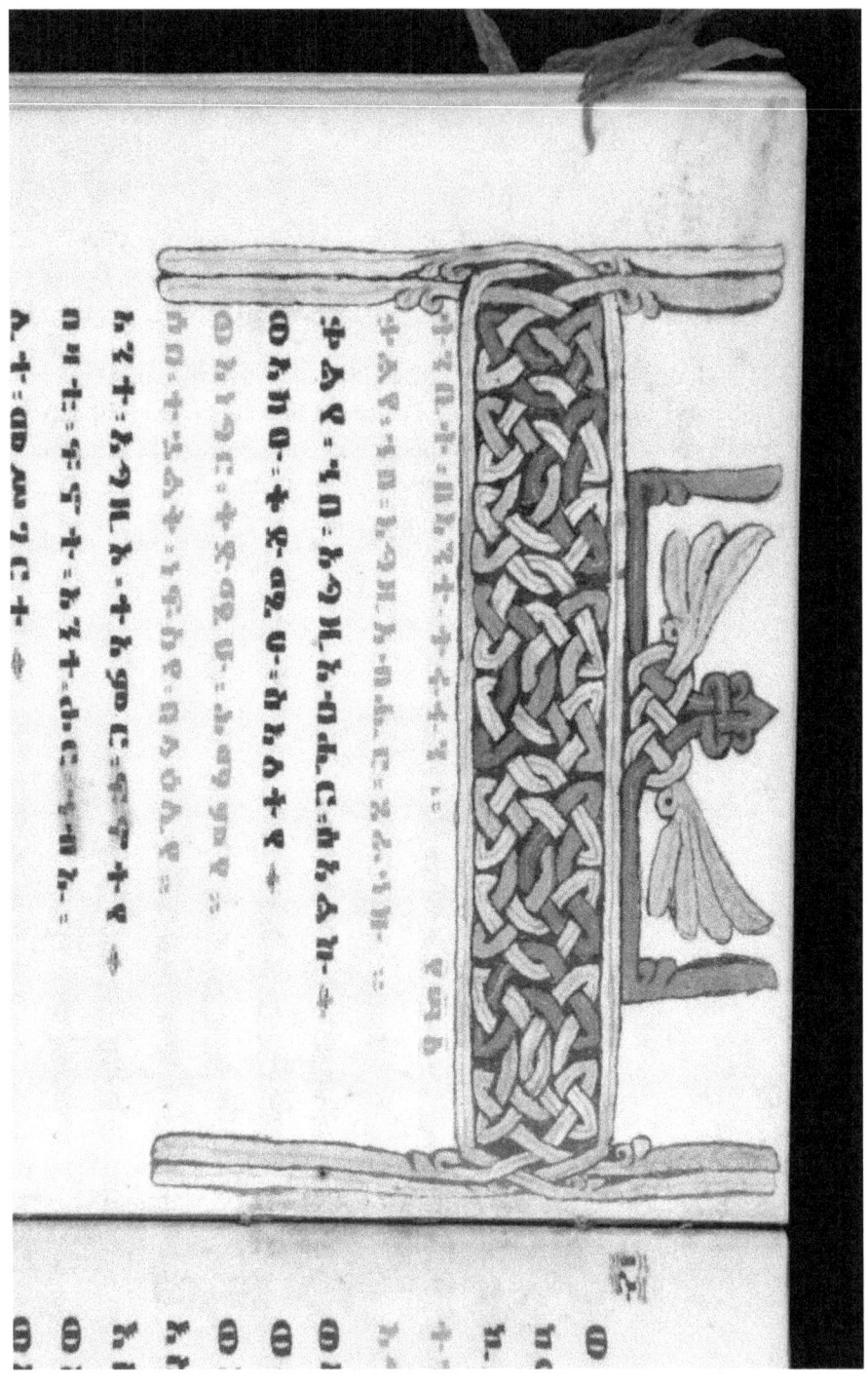

Plate 48: EMIP 44 (Eliza Codex 19), f. 140v

Plate 48: EMIP 44—Eliza Codex 19

So-called "deluxe" manuscripts will show not just one but an array of special characteristics. Usually the proportions, script size and margins are generous (though there are occasionally deluxe manuscripts where a small size seemed to be the desired characteristic). The quality of the parchment is fine and even throughout, with few if any holes. There is a high degree of scribal skill as evidenced, first, by the quality of the hand. In the case of this 20th century Psalter, there has also been careful planning and execution of the text layout: in the first three works not a single line of text had to be completed on a following line (something very rare indeed). A binding of tooled leather, complete with head and tail band, is another standard feature for the deluxe codex. Other features include the quality of the case (this one has a fine double-slip case), the presence of string navigation systems. This codex has fully eighteen of a theoretical nineteen possible *harägoč* (only the division between Praises of Mary and Gate of Light is unmarked). The presence of illuminations might be a final indication of deluxe status. This codex originally had no illuminations though eight have been added recently by "the speckled garment artist."[16] This picture shows the *haräg* that marks the section of ten psalms that begin at Psalm 141 (f. 140v). One can also see quire number (right) and strings (left). This codex shows almost no signs whatsoever of wear.

---

[16] It is not impossible that the specked garment artist was employed by the original scribe to add illuminations to this codex—as the part of the original production of the book. The entire manuscript was produced very recently.

Plate 49: EMIP 45 (Eliza Codex 20), ff. i v(erso)–1r

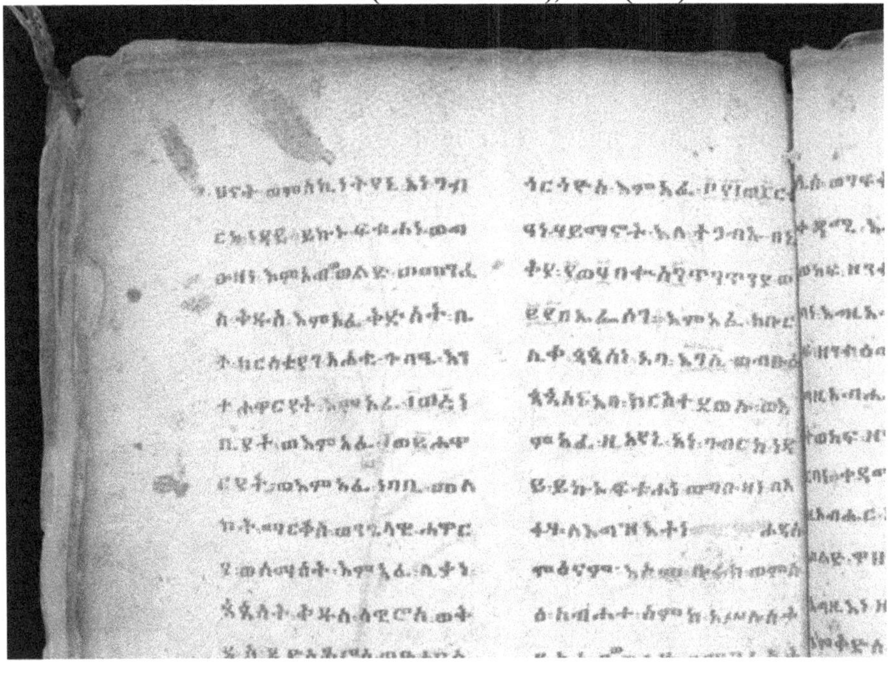

Plate 50: EMIP 46 (Eliza Codex 21), f. 8v

Plate 49: EMIP 45—Eliza Codex 20

The classic works of the Ethiopian Orthodox church are in Gəʻəz. Consequently, it is not very common to come across manuscripts written in Amharic. Perhaps the most frequent one would be manuscripts that contain the Amharic Commentary on Our Father. Besides the commentary (ff. 1r–41v), this 19th century codex also contains notes on orders of the rite of baptism and the Mass in Amharic (ff. 41v–42v, with other folios covered over with paintings). This codex has had a complete set of eight illuminations added by the speckled garment artist and marked with long brown yarn sewn into the fore edge of the folios with illuminations.

Plate 50: EMIP 46—Eliza Codex 21

On folio 8v, this Missal mentions Metropolitan Krestodolu enabling us to date the manuscript in the timeframe 1720–1743 A.D. The codex is worn and has undergone many repairs including a complete reweaving of the chain stitches, though this time with only three stitches. Several of the anaphoras between folios 26r–65v are rebound in total disorder. This photograph shows the name of the Metropolitan in column 2, line 6. But it also shows how the repairs to the codex have left much of the material at the gutter difficult to see. In the upper right corner of the picture is visible a stab stitch which is often used in repairs to repair quires that are falling apart. When these are used, much of the gutter is lost and the quire will no longer open to its full size.

Plate 51: EMIP 47 (Eliza Codex 22), f. 57r

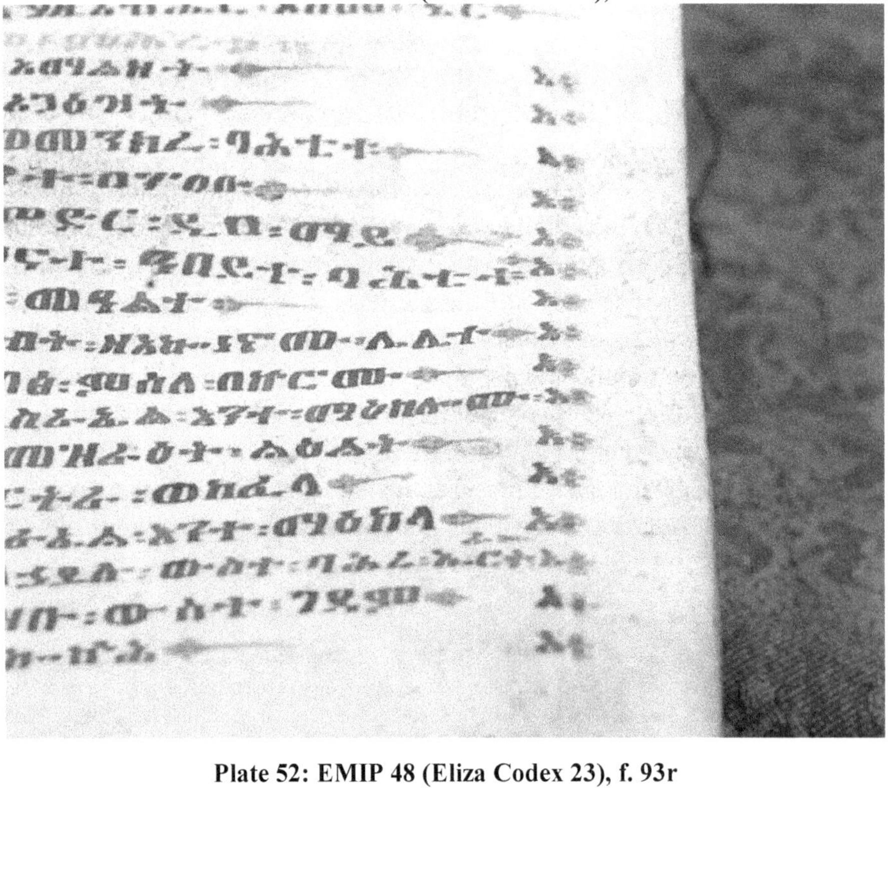

Plate 52: EMIP 48 (Eliza Codex 23), f. 93r

Plate 51: EMIP 47—Eliza Codex 22

The visual themes in *harägoč* from older manuscripts are limited mainly to interwoven vines and geometric patterns. More recent manuscripts sport *harägoč* with a number of other visual themes. This 20th century Psalter employs floral patterns, interwoven vines, eyes, human faces, woven crosses, and even snakes, the theme shown in Plate 51 (f. 57r).

Plate 52: EMIP 48—Eliza Codex 23

The 135th psalm (136 in the Hebrew Bible and English translations) is composed with a repeated response: "O give thanks to the LORD, for he is good, for his steadfast love endures forever. O give thanks to the God of gods, for his steadfast love endures forever. O give thanks to the Lord of lords, for his steadfast love endures forever" (vv. 1–3, NRSV). Regardless of age, just about every Ethiopic Psalter will lay out the page as shown in this plate. The letter on the right is to signify the repeated phrase, "for his steadfast love endures forever." The full-stop symbol is the distinctive form used in the late 19th and early 20th centuries.

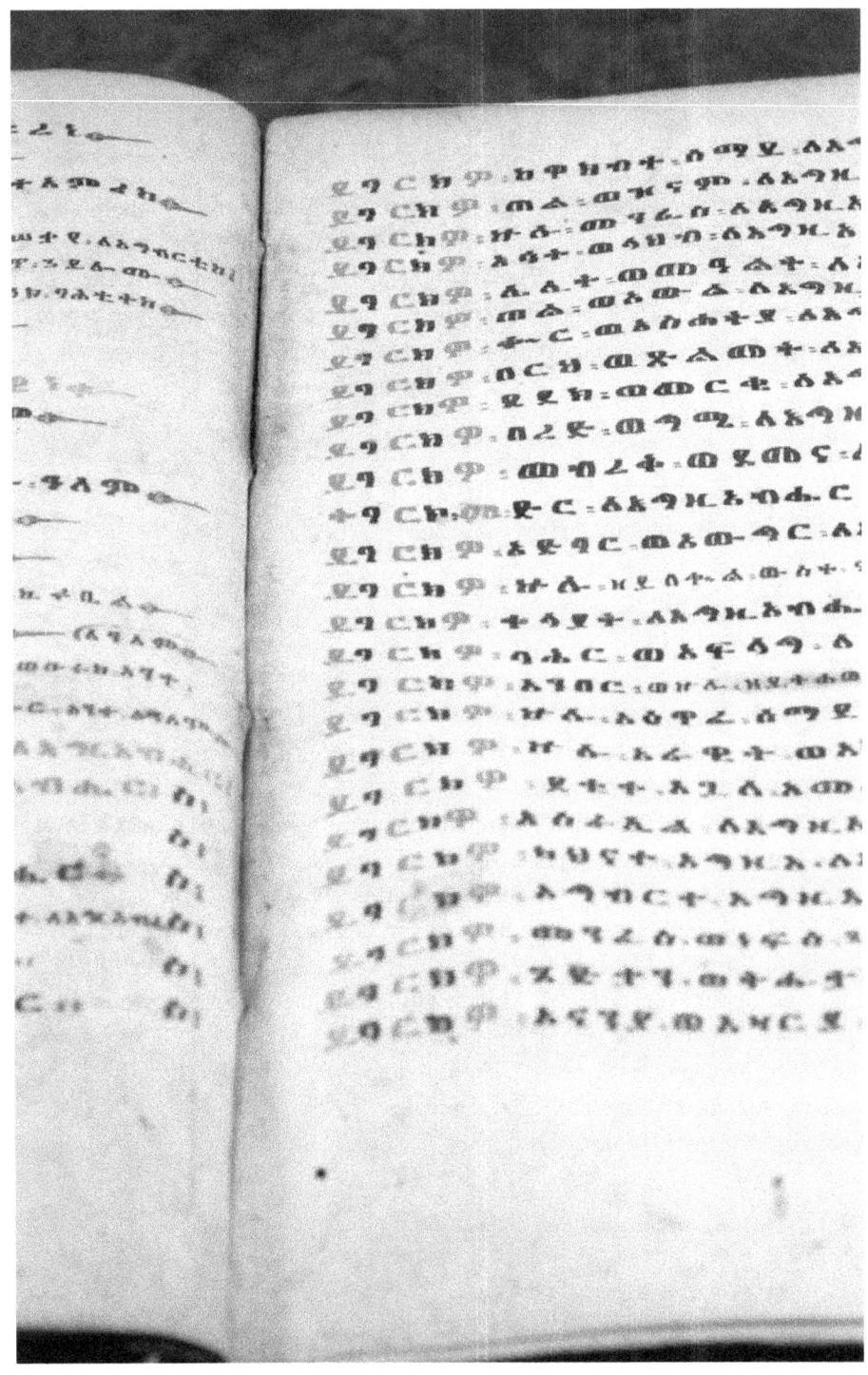

Plate 53: EMIP 49 (Eliza Codex 24), f. 112r

Plate 53: EMIP 49—Eliza Codex 24

The Biblical Canticles include biblical texts from all parts of the Ethiopian canon, included the so-called deutero-canonical texts. The tenth of these Biblical Canticles is the third song of the three young children, recorded in (the Additions to) Daniel 3:57ff (also known as the Prayer of Azariah 1:35ff). All the lines of this prayer begin with the same phrase: Bless the Lord, all you works of the Lord; sing praise to him and highly exalt him forever. Bless the Lord, you heavens; sing praise to him and highly exalt him forever. Bless the Lord, you angels of the Lord; sing praise to him and highly exalt him forever" (vv. 57–59). Regardless of age, most extant Ethiopic Psalters will lay out this canticle in a columetric format with the first word written in alternating red and black ink.

86 · *Ethiopian Scribal Practice 1*

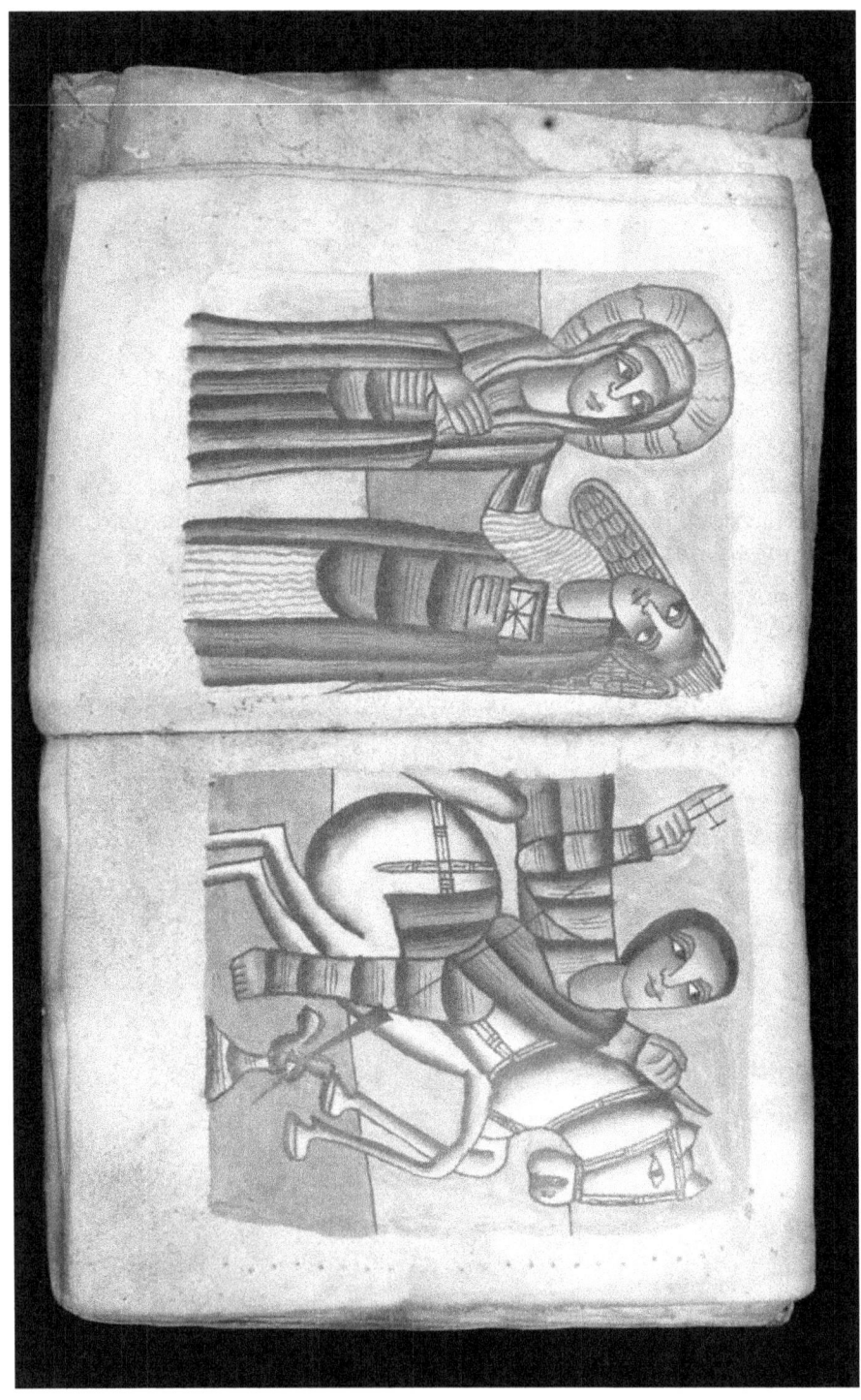

Plate 54: EMIP 50 (Eliza Codex 25), ff. 3v–4r

Plate 54: EMIP 50—Eliza Codex 25

Success breeds competition. Dealers of Ethiopian books have long known that books with illuminations sell better than books without. This plate shows the artwork of one we refer to simply as "the beautiful artist." We have every reason to believe that this person is a contemporary and competitor of "the speckled garment artist." The work of the "beautiful artist" adorns more than a dozen manuscripts that have come through our project. The illuminations are characterized by a lack of any border, a full background of color (to cover over the text) and very distinctive renditions of traditional artistic themes. On these folios of this 19th century Psalter we have the annunciation (left) and Saint George and the Dragon (right).

Plate 55: EMIP 51 (Eliza Codex 26), where quires 7 and 8 meet (ff. 67v–68r)

Plate 55: EMIP—Eliza Codex 26

The codex is another case where quires from various sources and from various times in the 19th and 20th centuries, have been collected into one book. Part One. Quires 1–5 contain the Five Pillars of Mystery, in Amharic (ff. 1–47). The text is all by one scribe, there are quire numbers for each quire, the page layout is in two columns, the top margins are 20 mm, bottom margins 36 mm, fore edge margins 20 mm, and gutter margins are 10 mm. There is one additional and secondary hand in quires 1 and 2. This hand writes in light black ink with a very small tip and makes notes between the main lines of text. These are visible in ff. 1r, 2r, 2v, 3v, 4v, 11r, and 11v. Part Two. Quires 6–7 contain Mystery of the Resurrection (ff. 48–67). The text is written in a new hand, there are no quire numbers, the page layout is in two columns, the top margins are 15–25 mm (irregular), bottom margins 35 mm, fore edge margins 10–15 mm, and gutter margins 5–7 mm. Part Three. Quires 8–9 contain a Hymn to Mary (ff. 67v–69v), and Admonition (ff. 70r–86v). The quire dimensions are shorter in height than the rest, there is a new hand, the page layout is in one column of 17 lines of text, the top margins are 8–10 mm, bottom margins 45 mm, fore edge margins 10 mm, and the gutter margins 12 mm. Part Four. Quires 10–11 contain the Amharic Commentary on Our Father (ff. 88r–97v), The Amharic Commentary on Hail Mary (ff. 98r–99r), Wise Saying in Amharic (ff. 99v–100v) and a Hymn to God (ff. 100v–101v). There is a new hand, the page layout is in one column of 18 or 19 lines of text, the top margins are 13–15 mm, bottom margins 32–35 mm, fore edge margins 5–8 mm, and gutter margins 10–13 mm. This plate shows the point where quires 7 and 8 meet in the codex. Quire 8 is clearly shorter.

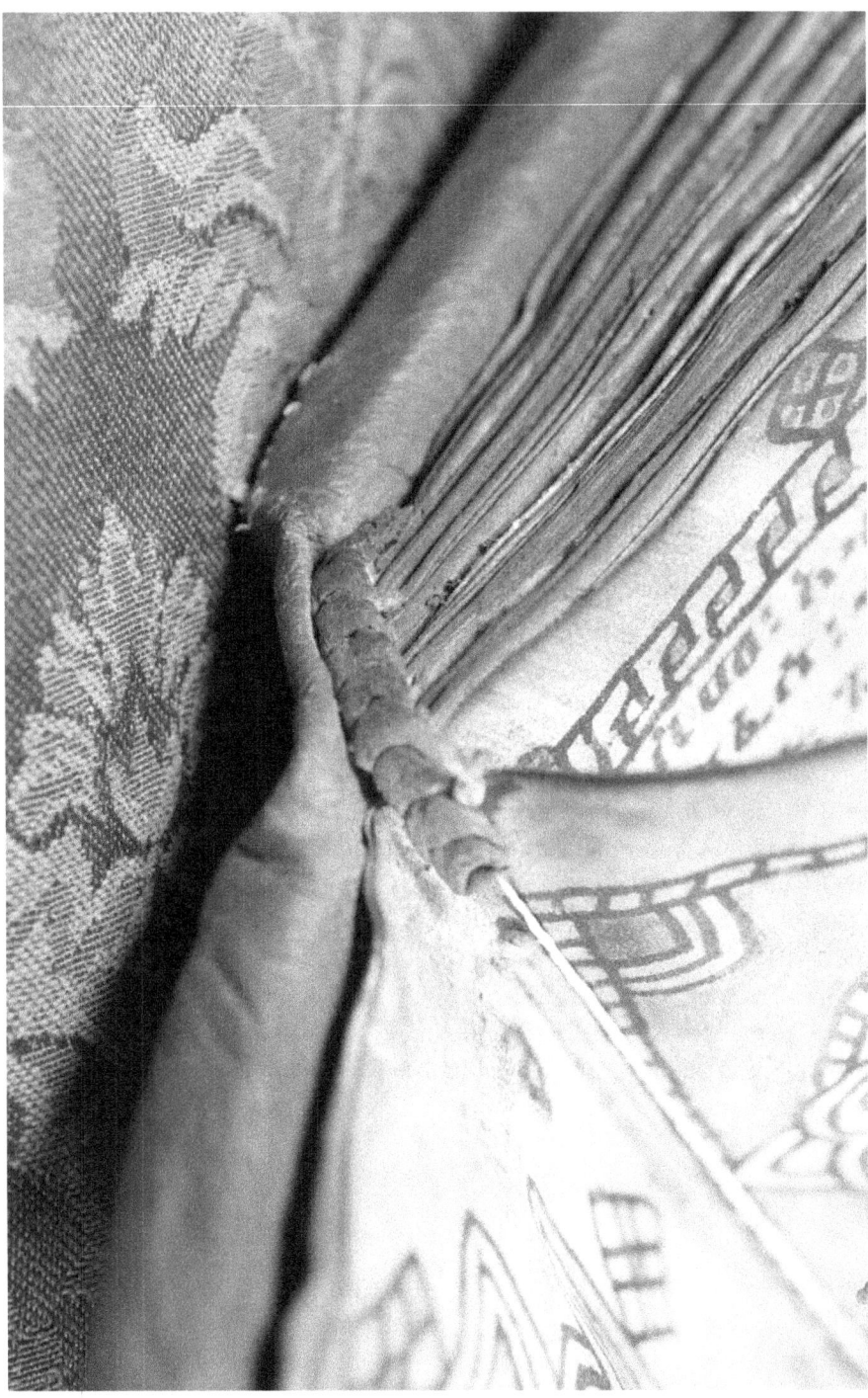

Plate 56: EMIP 52 (Eliza Codex 27), ff. ii v(erso)–iii r(ecto), upside down

Plate 56: EMIP 52—Eliza Codex 27

This 19th/20th century codex containing the Prayer of Mary at Golgotha, has a leather cover with head and tail bands. This image (taken from a perspective above the top edge of the book) shows a string that is tied between the ends of head band and tail band apparently to provide one more point of stabilization in the book. There are a few, but only a few, other codices with this feature.

Plate 57: EMIP 53 (Eliza Codex 28), ff. ii v(erso)–1r

Plate 57: EMIP 53—Eliza Codex 28

This codex contains a fairly rare work, *God Reigns* Ascribed to Zär'a Ya'əqob, copied in the 18th century. As much as we may respect the industry and ingenuity of modern artists bringing "aftermarket improvements" to old Ethiopic books, it is in a manuscript such as this that we see the problems involved with the practice. Three of the eight illuminations (ff. 11r, 31r and 51r) are painted over the top of the text of *God Reigns*. In the case of the two illuminations painted over the text of one of the *Miracles of Mary*, the loss is less crucial, since there are many more copies of the *Miracles of Mary*. Perhaps the greatest losses are caused, though, by the three illuminations painted over the end pages, folios i r(ecto)–ii v(erso). This is because it is often the end pages where we find the one-of-a-kind notes and Records and transactions, etc., recorded. This image yields one other interesting insight. We notice that this particular painting by "the speckled garment artist" is missing its speckles, the only one of the eight illuminations without them. At the very least, this points to the division of the painting process into steps, one of which was overlooked in this case, by the artist themselves. But, it is also possible that this oversight points to a division of labor in the artistic shop, in which an assistant, or apprentice, was given a codex whose basic paintings had been completed and their job was to add the speckles to the garments in order to finish the illuminations. The presence of apprentices with scribes is not rare at all as the next plate shows.

94 · *Ethiopian Scribal Practice 1*

Plate 58: A scribal school in Iste, Ethiopia in May of 2004

Plate 58: A Scribal School in Gondar

This plate shows a scribal school in Iste in southern Gondar to the East of Lake Tana.[17] The photograph was taken in May 2004, when I was traveling through Ethiopia with my translator and friend, *Ato* Daniel Alemu. Daniel was part of the Ethiopian community living in Jerusalem and I took him with me from Israel to Ethiopia when I went there to study more about the social location, education and economic engines surrounding the work of scribes. In order to locate schools of scribes to interview, we made use of the two small books published in 2002 by John Mellors and Anne Parsons, *Ethiopian Bookmaking* and *Scribes of South Gondar* (London: New Cross Books). Inside the back cover of both is a map detailing the "location of churches where working scribes can be found." John and Anne, whom I later met in London, had made three trips to the area between November 2000 and July 2002. Using their maps, we found this scribe, *Merigita* Hulgizé Nurilign (inset and standing in the center holding the manuscript), and his school. In white cloaks (on the scribe's right and standing to the far right of the picture) are older apprentices. Around them (many cloaked in blue uniforms) are the younger students and apprentices. The inset shows a closeup of the scribe holding Mellors and Parsons' book open to the page that has his picture on it.

---

[17] Sergew (BIE, pp. 28-29) discusses the setting in which students were trained to be scribes. In addition, see O'Hanlon, *Features of the Abyssinian Church*, pp. 13ff.

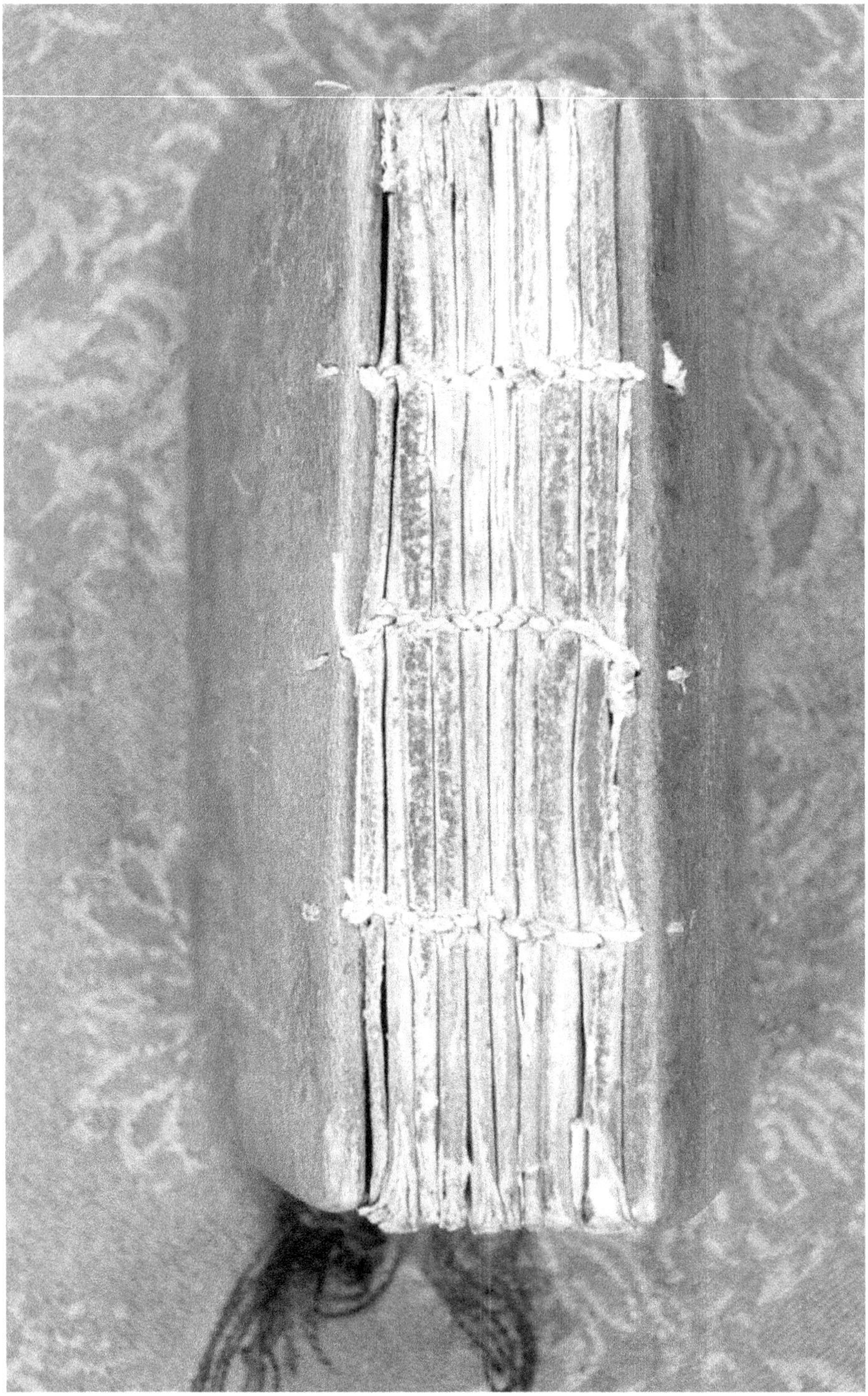

Plate 59: EMIP 54 (Eliza Codex 29), spine

Plate 59: EMIP 54—Eliza Codex 29

Well over 95% of the codices in our project have bindings with four sets of stitches, actually two pairs. In a few cases where a codex has been rebound, the new binding is in three stitches. In such cases, one can see plainly the location of the original stitching furrows in the spine of the book and how the new stitches are in different locations. This 19th/20th century copy of *Anaphora of Our Lady of Cyriacus of Bəhənsa* and *Prayer of Mary at Golgotha* is one of only a few with an original binding in three stitches.

Plate 60: EMIP 55 (Trinity Western University Codex 1), ff. 119v–120r

Plate 60: EMIP 55—Trinity Western University Eth. Ms. 1

As we have seen, many of the illuminations present in manuscripts that have come to North America are "aftermarket improvements" (some would use the term "forgeries"), designed at increasing the value of the book for sale, probably to tourists or other foreigners. There are fully ten illuminations in this 19th/20th century Psalter, but there are mixed signals about the provenance of the illuminations in relation to the original codex. On the one hand, there is an illumination (f. 130v) of *Abba* Qerəlos who was Archbishop of Ethiopia in the 1920's. This would suggest a time for the illuminations that is roughly contemporaneous with the production of the manuscript. On the other hand, in every case the miniatures are painted on parchment folios that are of a slightly different size than the surrounding folios. Further, the artist seems unfamiliar with certain key aspects of Ethiopian Orthodox art history. For one thing, the name of Mary is spelled differently than is normal in the tradition. Second, and much more serious, is the fact that Mary is painted in profile and showing only one eye. This practice of painting in profile, showing only one eye, is the standard way in which evil people are depicted. It seems unlikely that an illumination that deviates in such ways would be sold to one intimately familiar with the tradition.

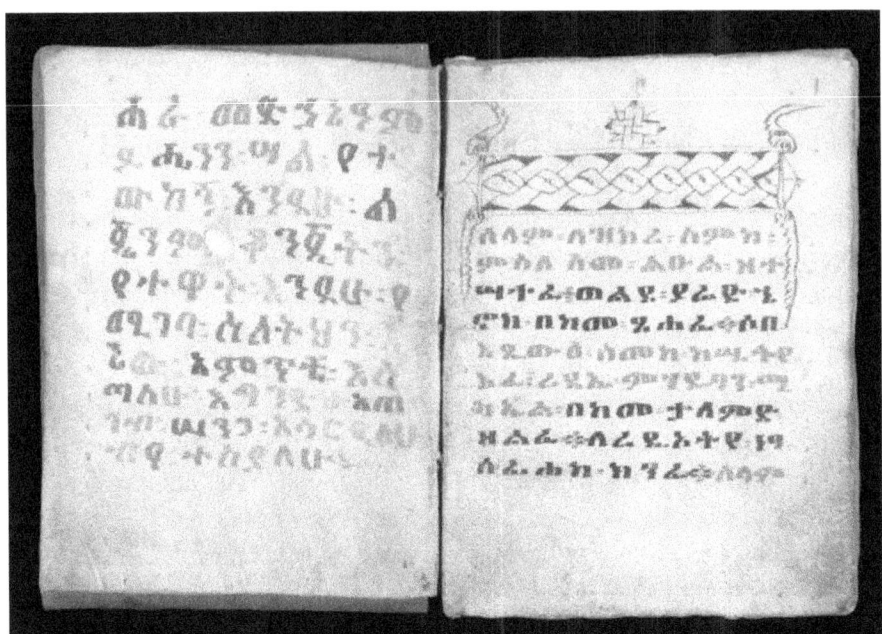

Plate 61: EMIP 56 (Trinity Western University Codex 2), ff. ii v(erso)–1r

Plate 62: EMIP 57 (Trinity Western University Codex 3), remains of codex with Canadian two dollar coin

Plate 61: EMIP 56—Trinity Western University Eth. Ms. 2

This plate shows another example of unique material that appears in the end sheets of these manuscripts. Folio ii v(erso) records a vow to kill a cow for Ḥara Mädḫane ʻAläm church if the person who vowed and his/her daughter are healed from the cough. Several other features of this 19th century book of Images are also visible: 1) the *haräg* on folio 1r which appears above the first major work, Image of Michael; 2) lines 1, 2, 5 and 6 written entirely in red ink; 3) the join (in the gutter) between the protection sheet (ff. i r[ecto]–ii v[erso]) and the first full quire; and 4) another example (in the gutter) of a codex with three binding stitches.

Plate 62: EMIP 57—Trinity Western University Eth. Ms. 3

This 17th century Psalter has suffered the loss of cover and many of its sheets. However, the fifty folios that remain span from Psalm 93 (missing Psalms 118–144) through Biblical Canticles, the Song of Songs and the first folio of Praises of Maryam, indicating that this Psalter originally included all the works in a standard Psalter.

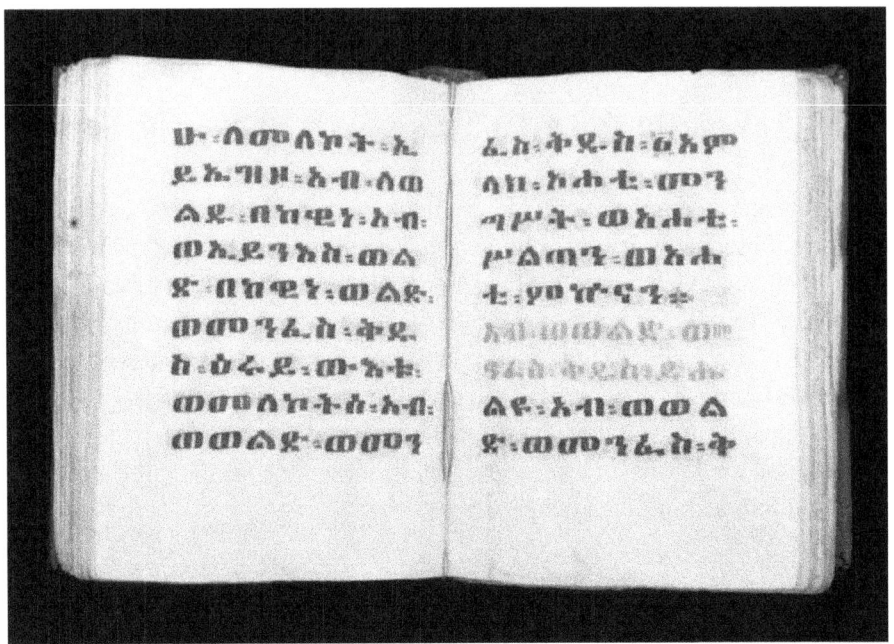

Plate 63: EMIP 58 (Tsunami Codex), ff. 28v–29r

Plate 64: EMIP 59 (Kahan Codex), upper spine and linen-lined cover

Plate 63: EMIP 58—The Tsunami Codex

This small (120 x 93 mm) 19th/20th century codex of the Anaphora of Our Lady Mary ascribed to Cyriacus of Bəhənsa, has many of the features of a deluxe, personal book: full covering of tooled leather, head and tail bands, beautifully copied large letters on few lines (9 lines per folio), fine parchment with no holes, etc. In the gutter, one can see not only the four binding stitches, but also the stitches that attach top and bottom of the quire to the head and tail band.

Plate 64: EMIP 59—The Kahan Codex

Thanks to the mention of Emperor Haile Sellassie (1930–1974) on folio 88r of this Missal, we know the general timeframe in which this manuscript was produced. One of the things that is interesting about the book is the unusual binding and cover. The quires are stitched together along four points in a chain stitch. However, the stitching does not attach to the board, as is usual in Ethiopic bindings. Instead, the cover appears to be a modified Islamic binding. The cover was made off the book without the envelope flap usual on Islamic bindings before 1700. The spine inside the case is covered in linen. The case was adhered to the book block with hinge linings. It has neither head nor tail bands.

104 · *Ethiopian Scribal Practice 1*

Plate 65: EMIP 65 (Eliza Codex 30), f. 178v and back cover

Plate 65: EMIP 60—Eliza Codex 30

Several codices—like this 18th century Psalter (f. 178v)—contain the Calendar of the Apostles and Evangelists, the days of the year on which their saint days are observed. This plate also shows the fate of many wooden covers. The wooden board used for the back cover has split along the grain in two places. These have been repaired by drilling three small holes and stitching the boards together. The front board of this codex is likewise broken and all but 35 mm (the part nearest the gutter) is missing. Pieces of heavy cardboard have been sewn together and then attached to the remaining piece of wood to function as a replacement front cover.

Plate 66: EMIP 61 (Eliza Codex 31), f. 151v and back cover

Plate 66: EMIP 61—Eliza Codex 31

This 20th century Psalter has contains ten illuminations. Eight are the familiar work of the "speckled garment artist." But the first and last (ff. i r[ecto] and 151v) appear to be more or less original with the codex. The different artistic approaches of the two artists reveal something of their intent. The "speckled garment artist" always covers the entire surface of the illumination area with a heavy coat of paint in order to cover up any text below. This artist employs the parchment itself as the background color of the illumination, revealing no intention to hide anything. The content of this illumination is a common one in Ethiopian Orthodoxy: the Holy Trinity. Each member of the trinity holds a symbol of authority (often, in the tradition, it is the orb of the world). Often the garment that covers the Trinity is a single garment without separation, suggesting their essential unity. Above the Trinity in this illumination, is a caption: the Trisagion (holy, holy, holy), ancient hymn of the Orthodox churches.

Plate 67: EMIP 62 (Eliza Codex 32), ff. 75v–76r

Plate 67: EMIP 62—Eliza Codex 32

Occasionally a portion or all of a folio needs to be repaired or replaced. This plate shows the typical way in which parchment is spliced onto parchment. A thin strip of parchment is snaked through both pieces of parchment through a series of slits. One can see the difference in scribal hand between the two folios (original hand on the left; later hand on the right) both in terms of the formation of the letters, but also in terms of the full stop symbol at the end of each line. The particular folio being replaced/repaired is the first folio on the back half of the quire. Consequently, we can see the stitching at the center of the quire in the gutter.

110 · *Ethiopian Scribal Practice 1*

Plate 68: EMIP 63 (Eliza Codex 33), ff. 31v–32r

Plate 68: EMIP 63—Eliza Codex 33

The text block of this 20th century manuscript of the Amharic Commentary on Our Father is similar to that of EMIP 52. Interspersed between the five normal quires of three and four sheets, are single-sheets whose only content are illuminations. The illuminations are placed on the inner folios (e.g., 7v and 8r); the outside folios of the sheets are blank (e.g., 7r and 8v). The subjects of the illuminations are a combination of images of saints and talismanic symbols. In this plate we see pictures two very prominent saints venerated by the Ethiopian Orthodox Church: Gäbrä Mänfäs Qəddus (f. 7v) and *Abunä* Täklä Haymanot. The details in the illuminations are standard in the tradition and are related to particular events in their lives. In an act of devotion, Gäbrä Mänfäs Qəddus, whose name means "Servant of the Holy Spirit," is said to have stood staring at the heavens for seven months without blinking an eye. The devil, in the form of a raven, comes to peck out his eyes. He is able to communicate with animals and is befriended by 60 lions and 60 leopards, with which he is always pictured. He is usually pictured covered with hair which miraculously grew when he refused to protect himself from the cold. *Abunä* Täklä Haymanot ("Plant of Faith") is said to have stood in one place for years praying to the point that one of his legs fell off. He is also said to have grown six wings with which to fly like the angels.

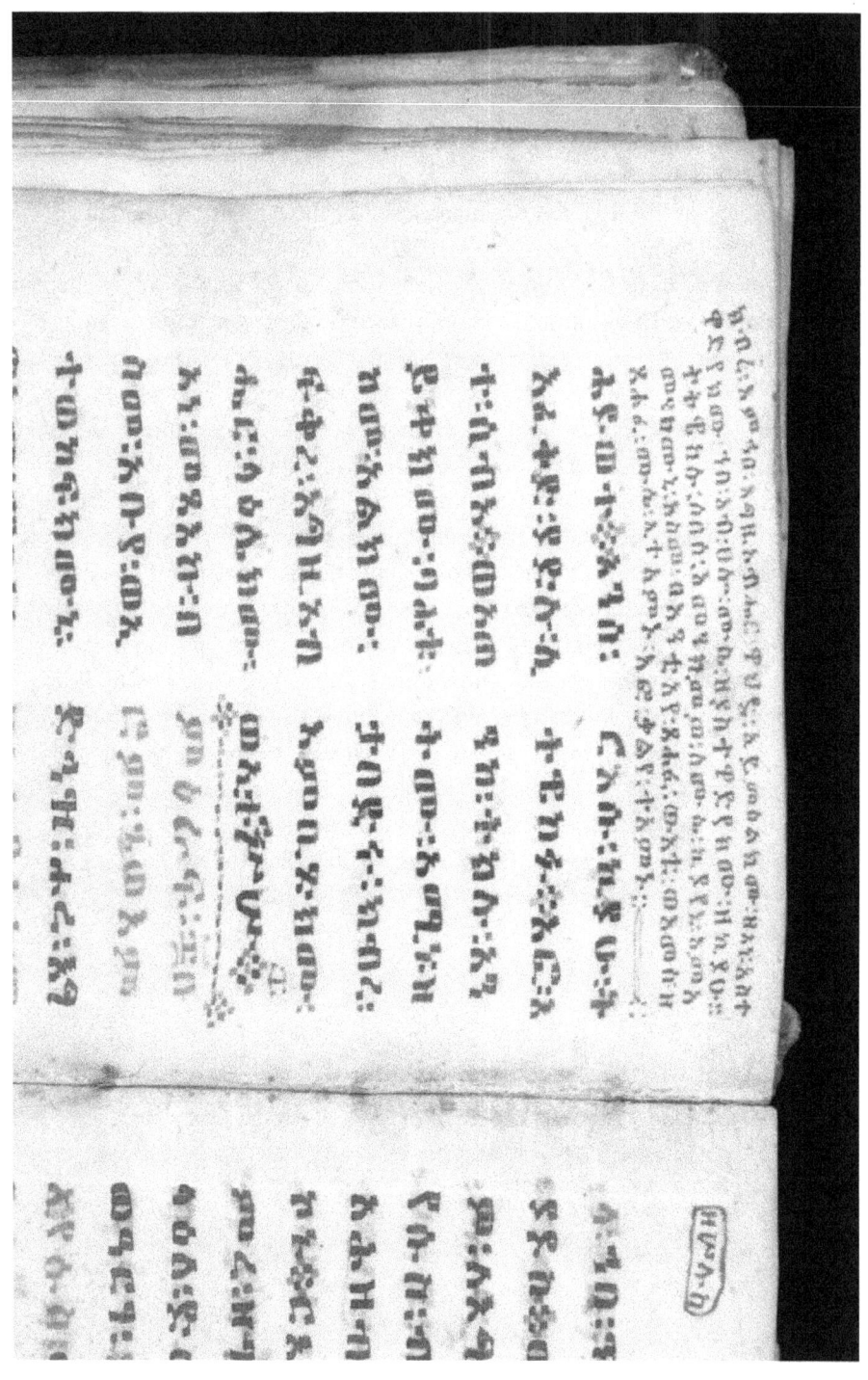

Plate 69: EMIP 64 (Eliza Codex 34), ff. 32v–34r

Plate 69: EMIP 64—Eliza Codex 34

Occasionally a scribe will leave out material or desire to insert additional material in a text that has already been completed. One way to address the problem is to insert the missing or added text into a marginal space and indicate with a mark in the text where it is to be inserted. In this 18th/19th century *Gospel of John* we see John 5:45–47 in the upper margin of folio 32v and a mark at the end of line 7 in column 2 where the text belongs. We can also observe one other scribal practice in this image. Some works are typically divided into sections for readings for the days of the week. Praises of Mary is always so arranged. The book of Psalms is sometimes arranged that way. The *Gospel of John* is usually arranged for the days of the week. A typical method for doing this is to place the name of the day of the week in the upper margin and circle the word in ink. Thus, we see "Tuesday" on the top of folio 33r.

114 · *Ethiopian Scribal Practice 1*

Plate 70: EMIP 65 (Eliza Codex 35), ff. 21v–22r

Plate 70: EMIP 65—Eliza Codex 35

As we have seen, *Praises of Mary* and *Gate of Light* are a standard part of Ethiopic Psalters. It is an indication of the centrality of these works in the life of the Ethiopian Orthodox community that *Praises of Mary* is copied in manuscripts that are not Psalters. This early 20th century manuscript contains *Praises of Mary* (ff. 1v–21v), *Gate of Light* (13v–20r) and the hymn, "The Angels Praise Mary" (ff. 20r–21v). The latter is not infrequently included in Psalters after *Gate of Light*. This plate shows the final portion of "The Angels Praise Mary" on folio 21v, the first nine lines. The remainder of that folio contains an *asmat* prayer against the devil (serpent), while the next (f. 22r) contains the beginning of the record of a transaction of goods which continues onto the verso of the same folio. The production values on this codex are not very high (small dimensions, cramped text on 23 lines, cover boards of non-traditional, wide-grained wood, etc.). But from the standpoint of the preservation of Ethiopia's book culture, it is a good thing to have works that represent the "bottom end" of the scale as well as those that come from higher social niches.

116 · *Ethiopian Scribal Practice 1*

Plate 71: EMIP 71 (Eliza Codex 36), exterior, linen book cover

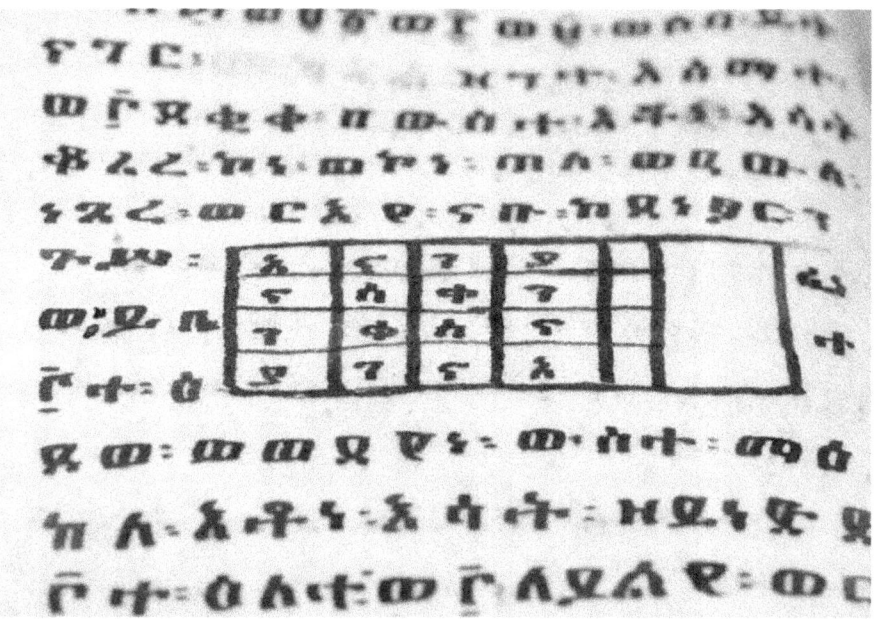

Plate 72: EMIP 67 (Focanti Codex 1), f. 88v

Plate 71: EMIP 66—Eliza Codex 36

Besides the *maḥdar*, leather boxes or cases, for the protection of books, Ethiopian books may also be protected with a cloth, double-pouch cover as seen in this plate. The long strip extending from the top of the spine is designed to wrap around the fore edge of the book and thereby cover and protect the text block from the elements. On the end of this strip is often placed a loop of string which reaches to the fore edge and secures the strap in place.

Plate 72: EMIP 67—Focanti Codex 1

This 19th century manuscript contains two works. The first is the very common Sword of the Trinity. The second is a collection of *asmat* prayers for the days of the week (ff. 42v–48v, 62r–100v and 101r–102v). At the heart of much of the thinking in Ethiopian magical texts, particularly the *Bandlet of Righteousness*, is a belief in the magical power of certain names. On folio 88v we see an example of an Ethiopian cryptogram that examines the name of one of the Israelite children in the fiery furnace, Ananiah. The story is told of the arrival of the archangel Michael to deliver them from the fire. He does so by uttering the magical numbers 39, 28 and 9, then the names given to them by God, at which point, the furnace became as dew, losing its heat. In the chart, the name is set forth as a palindrome (see Budge's preface to his *Bandlet of Righteousness*) in which the first row and the first column have the name forwards and the fourth column and the fourth row have the name backwards.

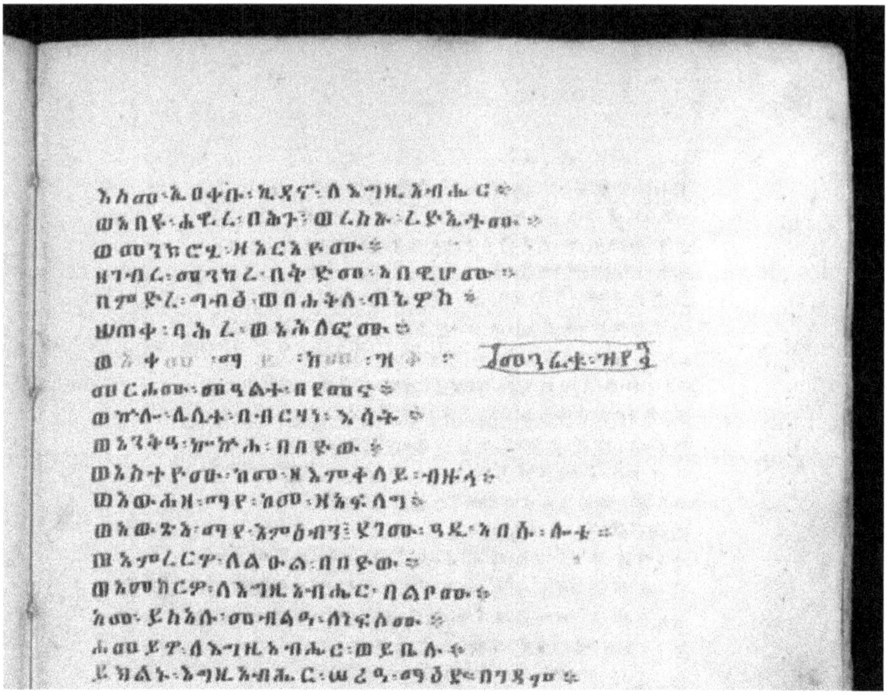

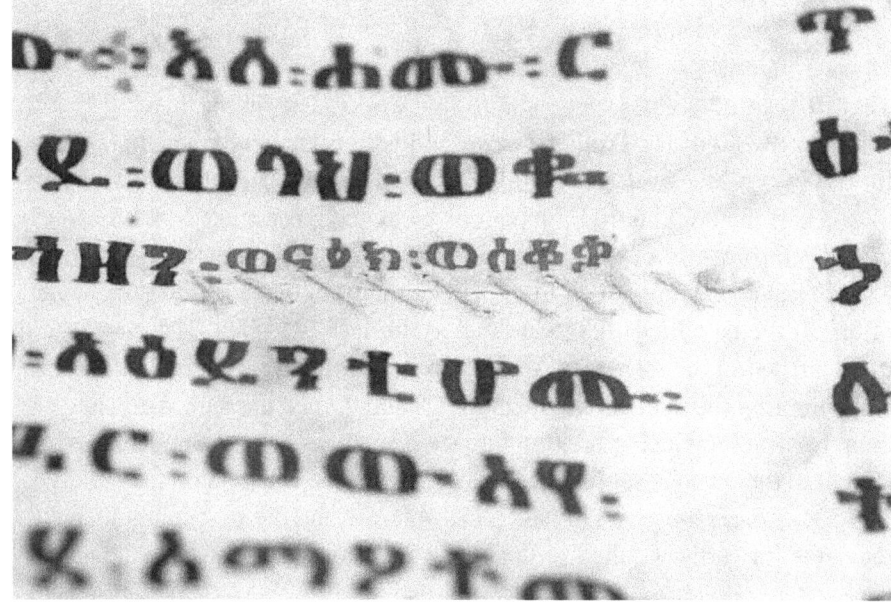

Plate 73: EMIP 68 (Focanti Codex 2), f. 64r

Plate 74: EMIP 69 (Focanti Codex 3), f. 108r

Plate 73: EMIP 68—Focanti Codex 2

Jewish scribes are known for their counting of words and for their calculations of such phenomena as the midmost of the words of the Torah or even the midmost of the letters of the Torah. Ethiopic Psalters frequently (ca. 48% of the time) have an indication of the midpoint of the book of Psalms, at Psalm 77:14 (ET 78:14). They mark this in various ways. EMIP 47 (Eliza 22), folio63v, has a symbol above a single word, "half." EMIP 61 (Eliza 31), f. 62v, contains four words in a box in the margin: "half [of it is] above; half [of it is] below." In this 18th century Psalter with the *Psalter of the Virgin*, the scribe has written the phrase "half (of it is) here" in a box in the margin. But they have also emphasized the line in the text by writing the letters in alternating red and black ink.

Plate 74: EMIP 69—Focanti Codex 3

We have seen that when parchment is torn or cut in the process of preparation, repairs are made with a wet stitch repair—the parchment is still wet as is the thin strip of parchment used as "thread." The whole dries and shrinks resulting in a tight repair that looks much like a scar. This plate shows a dry-stitch repair made to an 18th century *Funeral Ritual* after the original preparation and drying of the parchment—but before the text was written. The parchment appears to have broken along one of the scoring lines made to receive text. When too much pressure is applied during the process of scoring lines, the parchment can be weakened, or even cut, along the line. The parchment was sewn and text applied by a hand that "worked around" the repair.

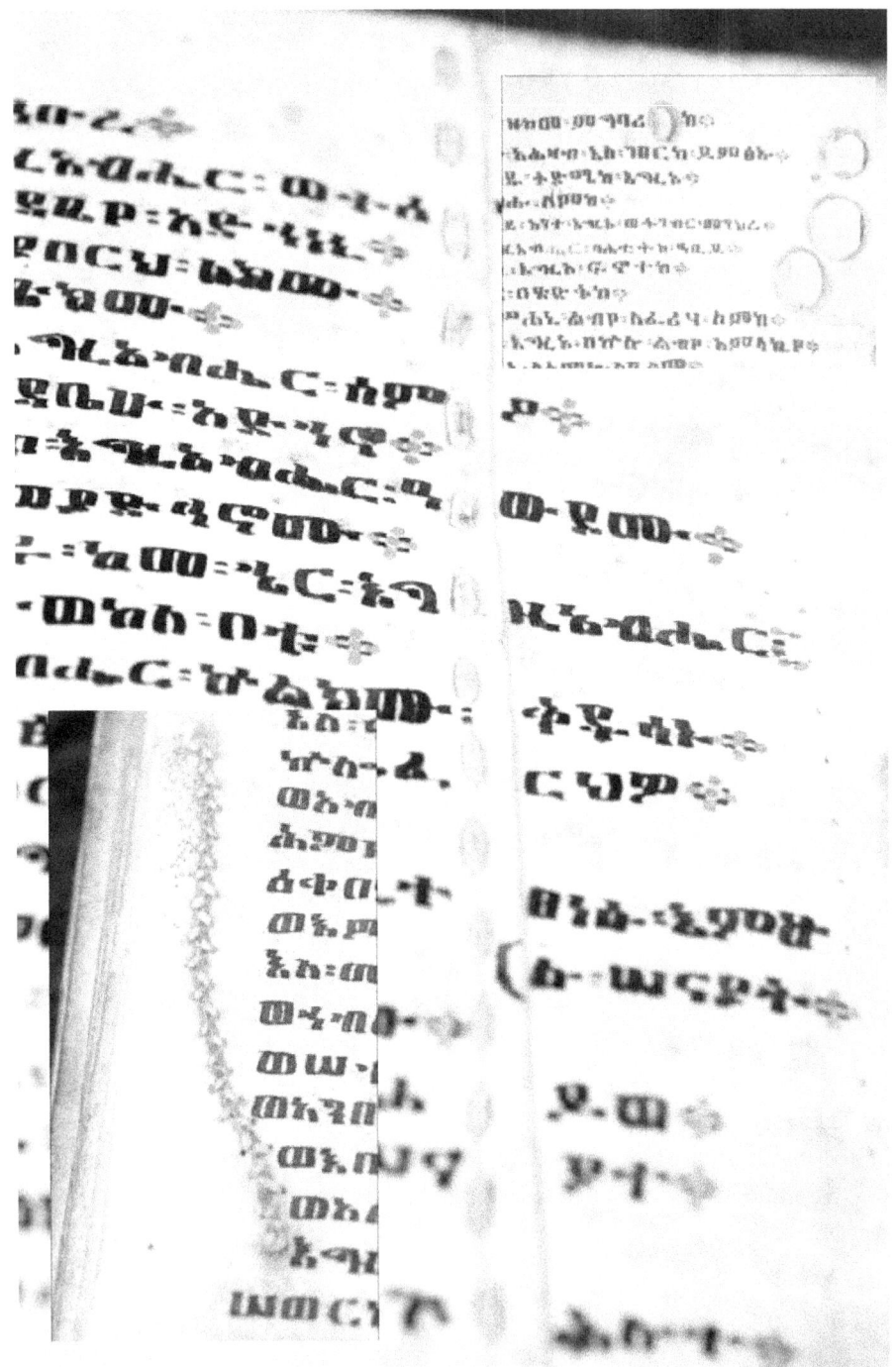

Plate 75: EMIP 70 (Marwick Codex 22), ff. 26r, 74r (top) and 120v (bottom)

Plate 75: EMIP 70—Marwick Codex 22

In Ethiopia, the value of the raw materials alone makes manuscripts inherently valuable objects. Assefa (*PPM*, p. 265) quotes a source in 1959 saying that the skins of twenty average-sized goats are required for a small-sized Psalter; a large Psalter would require thirty. And a four Gospels manuscript would require thirty to fifty goats. As in all markets everywhere, demand variegates the supply into a range of low-cost and high-cost options. Several scribal practices in this 20th century Psalter would seem to indicate an origin in a lower socio-economic niche. All available resources are pressed into service. Folios are spliced, repaired and used—even those with holes. In addition to materials, certain aspects of the workmanship point in the same direction. For instance, the hair follicles of the goats are clearly visible on many sheets in this manuscript, indicating less time spent in the preparation of the parchment.

Plate 76: EMIP 71 (University of Oregon Museum of Natural and Cultural History, Shelf Mark 10–845), f. 51v

Plate 77: EMIP 72 (University of Oregon Museum of Natural and Cultural History, Shelf Mark 10–843, f. 14r

Plate 76: EMIP 71—University of Oregon Museum of Natural and Cultural History, Shelf Mark 10–845

There are several ways in which scribes mark the divisions between sections: *harägoč*, lines of text written fully in red ink, lines of alternating red and black dots, a series of full-stop symbols, etc. The scribe in this 20th century Psalter has combined and innovated on standard themes (a rare feature of Ethiopian scribal practice) by weaving a line of alternating red and black dots around a series of full-stop symbols.

Plate 77: EMIP 72—University of Oregon Museum of Natural and Cultural History, Shelf Mark 10–843

The addition of musical notation requires special skills and training from a scribe. The small size of the interlinear musical notation—around 1 millimeter high in this case—requires a steady hand and a keen eye. This Missal was produced during the reign of King Täklä Haymanot I, who ruled from 1706 to 1708. His name is mentioned on folio 65v.

124 · *Ethiopian Scribal Practice 1*

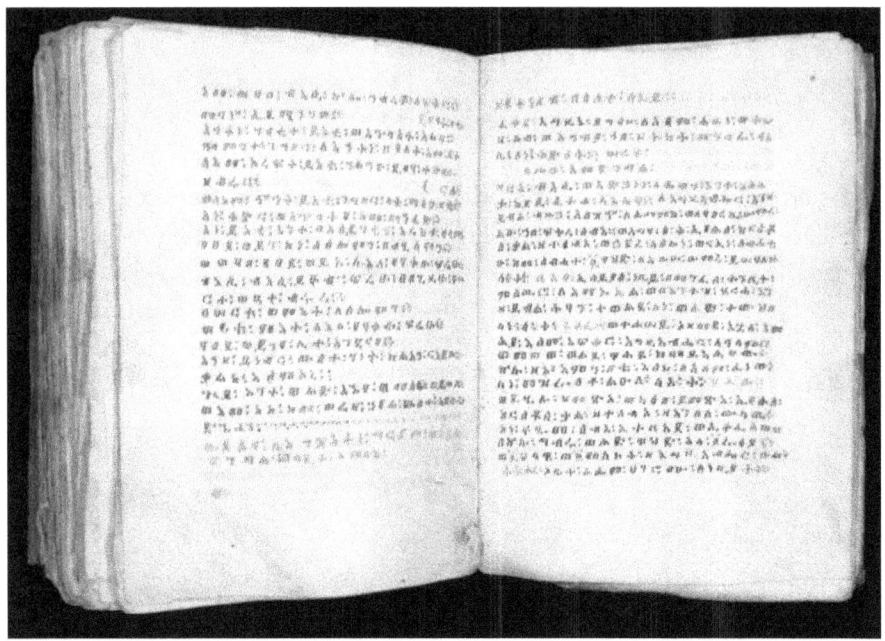

Plate 78: EMIP 73 (University of Oregon Museum of Natural and Cultural History, Shelf Mark 10–844), ff. 125v–126r

Plate 79: EMIP 73 (University of Oregon Museum of Natural and Cultural History, Shelf Mark 10–844), ff. 57v–58r

Plate 78: EMIP 73—University of Oregon Museum of Natural and Cultural History, Shelf Mark 10–844

There is hardly any practice more uniform in the Ethiopian scribal tradition than the page layout of the Psalter. As we have seen, the first three works of the Psalter are laid out in one column with each verse beginning on a new line and a full-stop ending each line. The last two works (*Praises of Mary* and *Gate of Light*) are laid out in two columns, each column right and left justified. This 20th century Psalter is one of only a few of the hundreds of Psalters that I have inspected that lays out the last two works in one column.

Plate 79 EMIP 73—University of Oregon Museum of Natural and Cultural History, Shelf Mark 10–844

The full-stop symbols on folio 57v (left) have been completed with red ink. The full-stop symbols on folio 58r (right) have not been completed. This small oversight indicates once again either the division of steps in the work process for the scribe who performs all of the steps himself, or, more likely, the division of labor between the scribe, who inserts the four black dots of the full-stop symbol as he writes the text, and his assistant, who adds four (or five) more dots in red ink to complete the full-stop symbols.

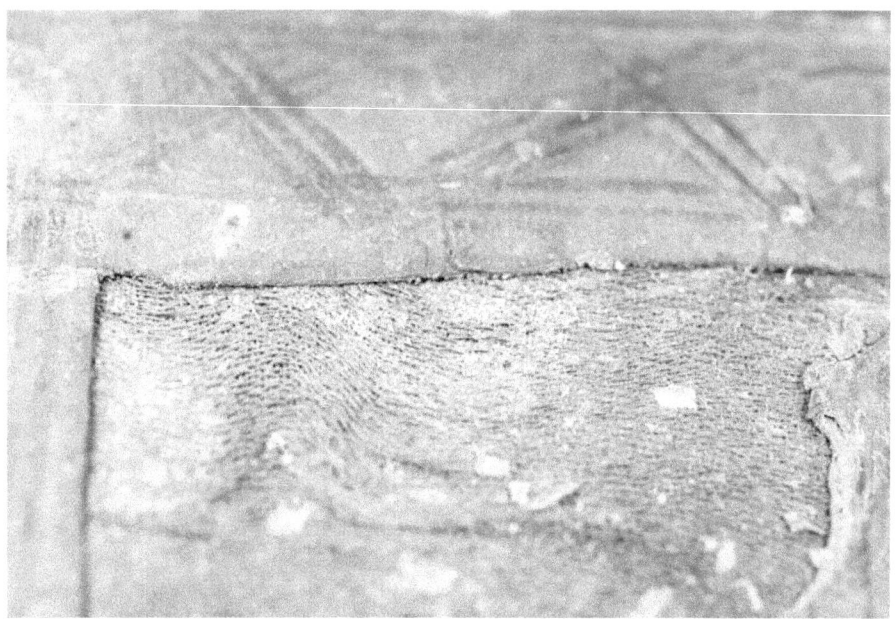

Plate 80: EMIP 74 (Mount Angel Codex), inside back cover

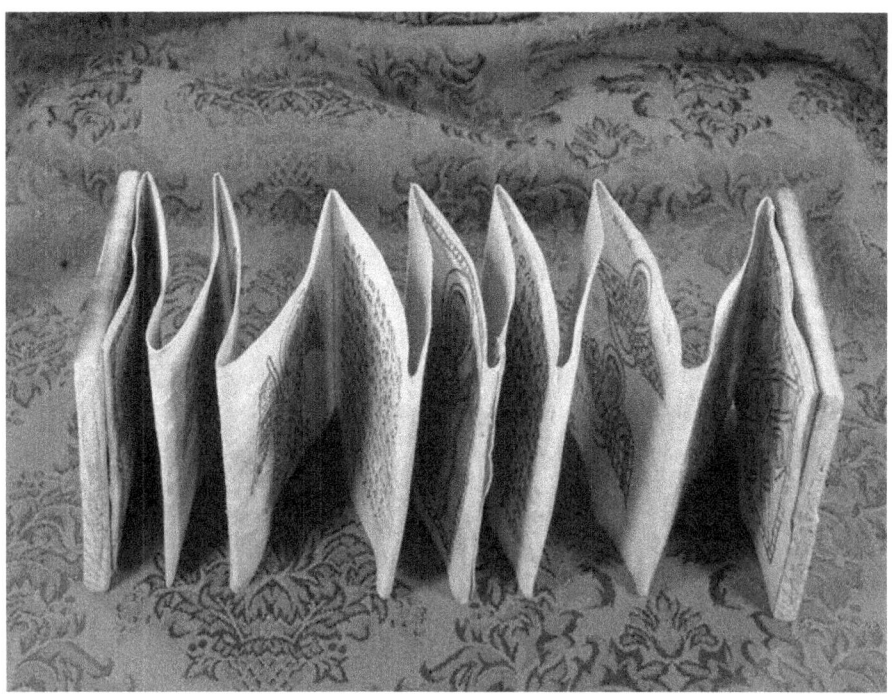

Plate 81: EMIP 75 (Weiner Codex 1)

Plate 80: EMIP 74—The Mount Angel Codex

Leather binding of a book is one of the clearest indicators of a higher socio-economic niche. With leather binding usually come several additional features to a book, including tooling of the leather, head and tail bands, and fabric used in certain places. When boards are covered with tooled leather, the leather is trimmed and pasted down to the inside of the front and back covers. In the rectangular space between the paste downs one will usually see a piece of colored cloth on the board. Since scholars can tell a great deal about the provenance of the book and its materials by the characteristics of the cloth used, we have taken care to photograph extreme closeups wherever cloth appears (between paste downs or in double-pouch book covers, etc.). The owner of this early 20th century book of Image of Gabriel, the Mystogogia and Bandlet of Righteousness can plausibly be identified as one *Ras* Berru, a governor in Ethiopia in 1932.

Plate 81: EMIP 75—Weiner Codex 1

A few Ethiopic books employ the "accordion fold book" format. These are usually small in their overall dimensions than most books and sometimes used as amulets. Further, their content is usually related to magical prayers and talismanic symbols.

Plate 82: EMIP 76 (Weiner Codex 2), f. 83v

Plate 82: EMIP 76—Weiner Codex 2

Perhaps the third most frequently-encountered Ethiopian book, after the Psalter and the Gospel of John, is the *Dərsanä Mika'el* or *Homiliary for the Monthly Feast of the Archangel Michael*. The work is laid out for the months of the year and for each month there are four elements: a homily, a story of one of the miracles of Michael, a story from the *Synaxary* (the Ethiopian book of Saints) about a miracle of Michael, and a concluding greeting. This 19th century copy contains a few full-color illuminations, but the vibrancy of the colors makes it clear that they have been added in the 20th century. The same may be said for this drawing on folio 83v. The iconic themes are very old and shared with the rest of the Christian world: Based on the scene in Ezekiel of the four living creatures around the throne of God, the Lord is seated on the throne, holding an orb. The four living creatures—which eventually come to be interpreted in the Christian world as the four Gospel writers (Matthew, the angel; Mark, the Lion; Luke, the Ox; and John, the eagle)—carry the throne of God. These shared iconic themes find their own unique expression in Ethiopia, but this particular artistic style is clearly a copy of a European original.

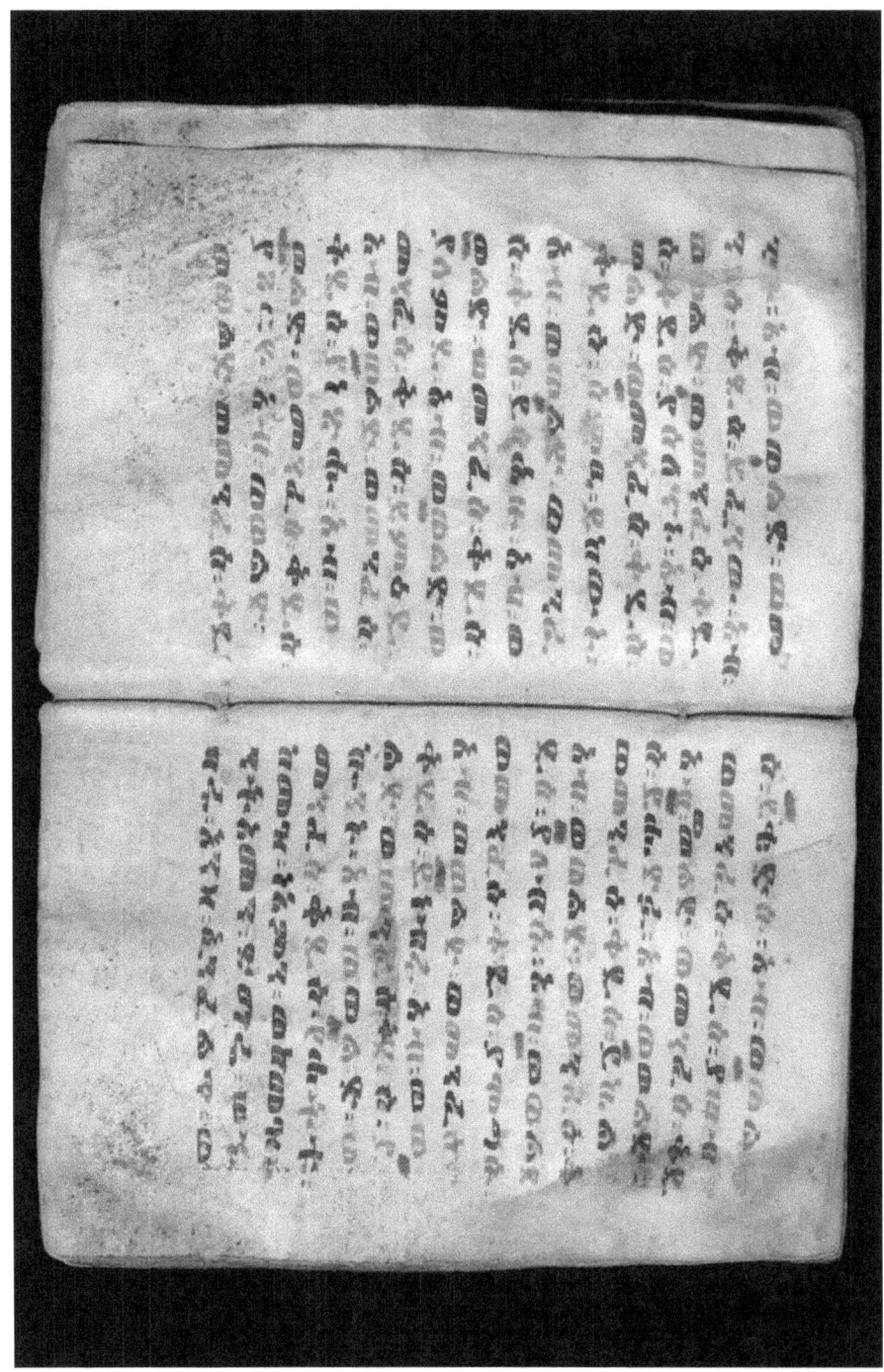

Plate 83: EMIP 77 (Bernhardt Codex), ff. 11v–12r

Plate 83: EMIP 77—The Bernhardt Codex

Theodore Bernhardt, Jr. of New Jersey has the distinction of being the first person to place a complete set of images of an Ethiopian manuscript online. This manuscript contains the *Anaphora of Our Lady Mary*, *Image of Mary* and the *Mystagogia* and was copied some time during the reign of Metropolitan Matewos (1889–1926), who is mentioned on folio 2v. The manuscript images have been available at http://members.tripod.com/~palaeography/index.html since 2002. This particular plate shows a scribal phenomenon on folios 11v–12r. We have seen how scribes will emphasize a text by writing the letters in alternating red and black ink. This passage is filled with Trinitarian formulae which are marked in this way.

Plate 84: EMIP 78 (Eliza Codex 37), ff. 8v–9r

Plate 84: EMIP 78—Eliza Codex 37

This 19th century manuscript contains the *Gospel of John*, *Canticle of the Flower*, *Lamentation of the Virgin* and *Image of Mary*. Somewhere in the late 20th century, a lovely set of eight illuminations were added over the top of the text. The illuminations capture traditional Ethiopian iconic themes. Here we see an image of the Holy Trinity surrounded by the four living creatures. As is usually the case, the Holy Trinity wears one garment, indicating the essential unity of the Trinity. In this case, the artist goes one step further and provides the Trinity with only five hands and has them holding both a holy book and an orb. The number of arms given to the Trinity varies between 4 and 6 among the Ethiopian artists in these codices. In the upper left corner of folio 9a we can see the quire number "2" which has been partially covered by the painter.

Plate 85: EMIP 78 (Eliza Codex 37), codex with spine strap

Plate 86: EMIP 79 (Eliza Codex 38), f. 11v

Plate 85: EMIP 78—Eliza Codex 37

This codex—and, perhaps five percent of the codices we have seen—has been outfitted with a spine strap. A single sheet of parchment wraps around all the quires. The cover boards are placed over the sheet and the strap is woven into the binding. Its purpose is to protect the spine from wear and to prevent dirt from collecting. In some cases, the sheet of parchment extends only a little wider than the spine (as is the case in the front of the book), or it can extend quite a ways towards the fore edge of the book (as is the in the back of this book and pictured in the left inset). In the latter case, the sheet provides another folio which may or may not receive text.

Plate 86: EMIP 79—Eliza Codex 38

As with most of the illuminations in these codices, the illuminations in this 20th century Psalter have been painted over text. This photograph shows the back side of a folio that was painted over. The folio was back-lighted and the text that is underneath the paint shows through on the back side in reverse.

Plate 87: EMIP 79 (Eliza Codex 38), f. 80v

Plate 87: EMIP 79—Eliza Codex 38

Although the illuminations are secondary, the *harägoč* in this manuscript appear to be original. This example shows the incorporation of angelic figures along with the more traditional interwoven patterns. Assefa (*PPM*, p. 263), writing in 1958, describes it as common practice for scribes to incorporate the head of an archangel or a cross into *harägoč*.

Plate 88: EMIP 80 (Eliza Codex 39), ff. 101v–102r

Plate 88: EMIP 80—Eliza Codex 39

In an environment of scarce resources, all available materials are pressed into service. The usual construction of a quire involves taking usually four or five sheets and folding them over to form a quire. But often scribes have a piece of parchment that is big enough for a folio, but not big enough for a full sheet. In such cases, the scribe will cut the sheet to a size that is about one centimeter wider than the folios in the codex. This half sheet is folded with the one centimeter of material on the other side of the gutter. This folio stub provides a way to include the folio into the quire and an anchor point for sewing into the book. The codices catalogued in this volume were made up of 1,201 "normal" quires (i.e., neither protection nor final quires). Fully 14.3% of these quires made use of half sheets with folio stubs. The quire pictures in this plate makes use of two half sheets, the net effect being that the quire has just as many folios and is balanced as a normal quire, i.e., with the same number of sheets on either side of the center of the quire. In these cases we refer to the quire as an "adjusted balanced" quire.

Quire 12: 99 100 101 102 103 104 105 106 107 108

Stubs appear between ff. 101 and 102 and between ff. 106 and 107.

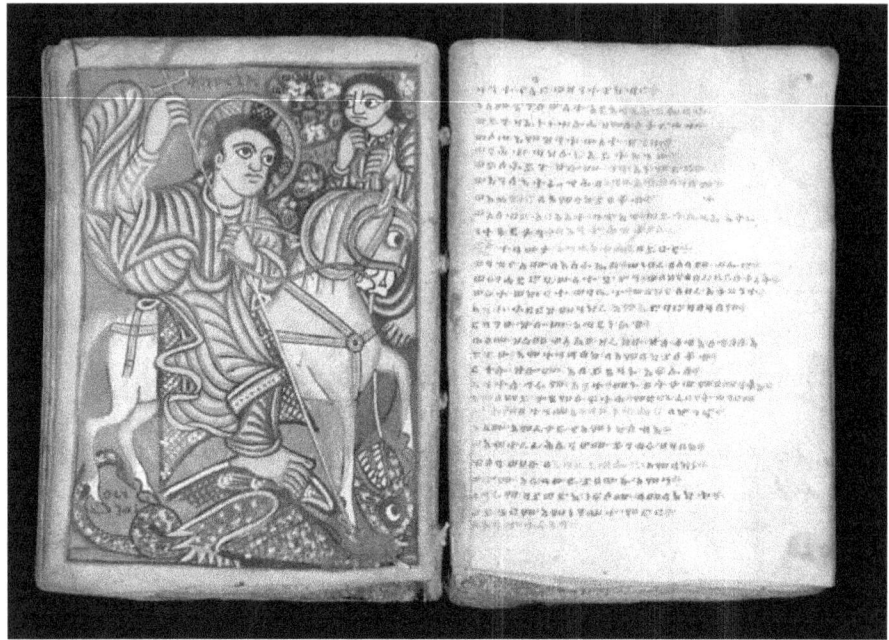

Plate 89: EMIP 81 (Eliza Codex 40), ff. 38v–39r

Plate 90: EMIP 82 (Eliza Codex 41), f. 36r

Plate 89: EMIP 81—Eliza Codex 40

This late-19th century Psalter (King Yoḥannəs [1872–1889] is mentioned on folio 93r) has been outfitted with a fresh set of illuminations. The interesting thing about these illuminations is that they are clearly by an artist other than the "speckled garment artist," and yet they share so many things in common with the "speckled garment artist." The content of the six illuminations are drawn from the standard icons used by the "speckled garment artist." Most of the details are identical. In some cases, the details are fuller and finer than those by the "speckled garment artist." And yet, certain details are different. For instance, there are no speckles on the garments, and the faces are drawn differently, etc. It seems likely that the two artists share a studio or that one is copying the other.

Plate 90: EMIP 82—Eliza Codex 41

This plate shows the sort of damage that water can do to a manuscript. In this case, the red ink seems to run worse than the black ink does. This early 20th century manuscript (Patriarch Yoḥannəs XIX [1928–1942], is mentioned on folio 41v) contains Prayer of Mary at Golgotha and Absolution of the Son as well as a few other minor works. The manuscript was copied for one Gäbrä Mädḫən (f. 36r and *passim*), whose name can still be made out at the end of line 5 and the first letter of line 6 despite the water stains.

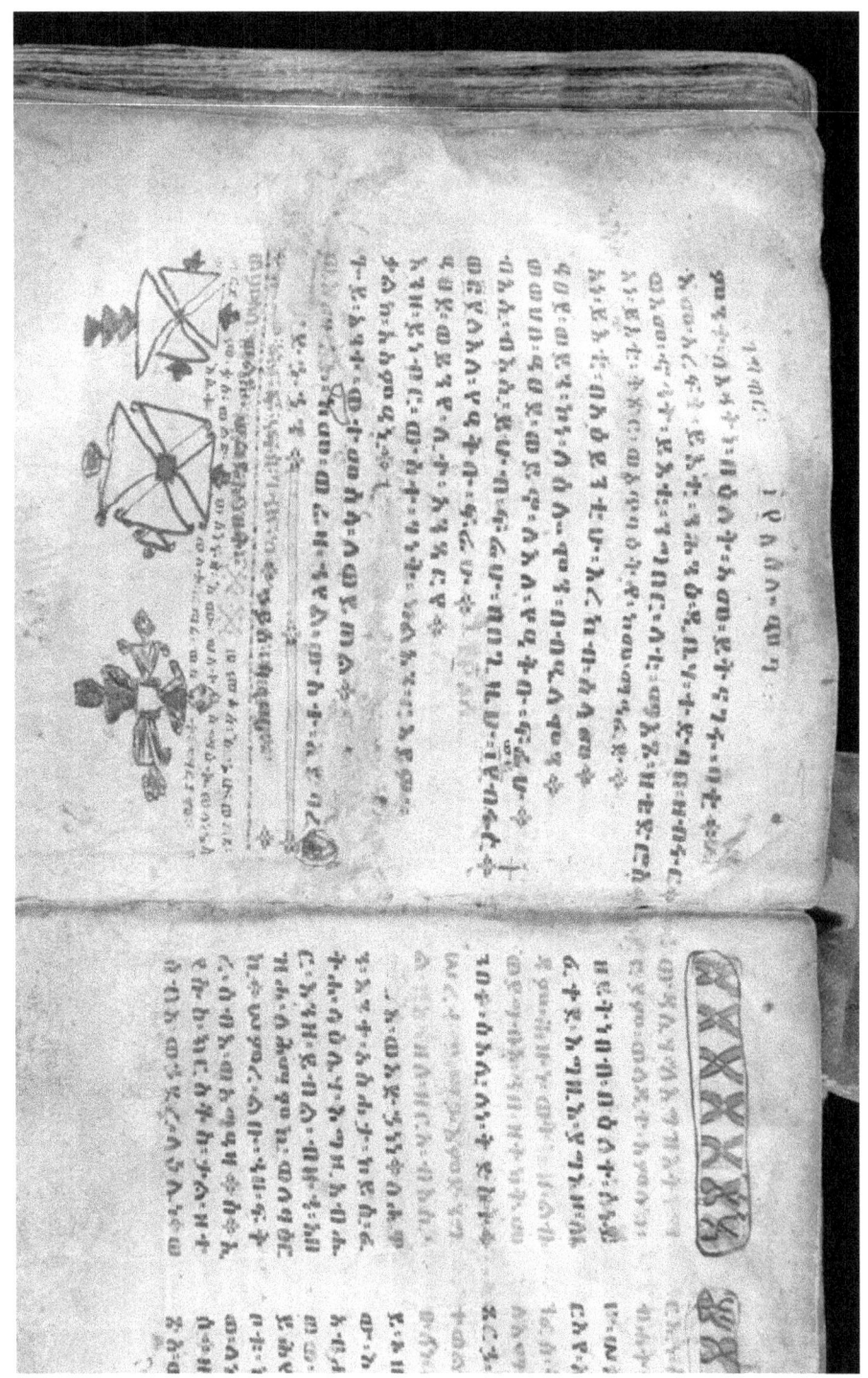

Plate 91: EMIP 83 (Weiner Codex 3), ff. 163v–164r

Plate 91: EMIP 83—Weiner Codex 3

This 18th century Psalter contains at least a half dozen *asmat* prayers: an illegible one on ff. i rv; one against the devil invoking the Trinity, Christ and the cross on folio i v(erso); one against the evil eye on folios i v(erso)–ii r(ecto), another illegible one on folio ii v(erso); one against stomachache on folio iii r(ecto); and another against the evil eye on f. 184v(erso). New owners of a manuscript will not only insert their own names over the names of previous owners, they will also update it in other ways. At the bottom of folio 163v, we see a prayer for the souls of many people. The names of the original people have been effaced and a new set of names has been inserted. In this image we see the conclusion of Song of Songs (left) and the beginning of Praises of Mary (right). In the upper margin we can also see a correction to the text to be inserted at the end of line eight (see the sign there).

144 · *Ethiopian Scribal Practice 1*

Plate 92: EMIP 84 (Delamarter Codex 2), exterior and amulet case

Plate 92: EMIP 84—Delamarter Codex 2

A fascinating aspect of Christian book culture is that some books were made not to be read, but to be worn. This practice was observed throughout the Christian world including Ethiopia This late 20th century copy of Bandlet of Righteousness is made to a tiny scale: 65 x 49 millimeters. It comes outfitted with an amulet case for wearing around the neck or under the arm. The amulet is worn for its inherent protective powers not so that the text will be ready at hand for reading. In this case, the small book has been crafted to fairly high production standards with a beautiful tooled leather cover and colorful linen visible between the paste downs inside the front and back covers.

Plate 93: EMIP 85 (Trinity Western University Codex 4), exterior unfolded

Plate 94: EMIP 86 (Marwick Codex 21), inside front cover and f. 1r

Plate 93: EMIP 85—Trinity Western University Eth. Ms. 4

This codex is another example of a 20th century amulet copy of *Bandlet of Righteousness*. Once again the dimensions are tiny (54 x 45 mm). But this time the format is an accordion-fold book. This manuscript was probably also worn as an amulet.

Plate 94: EMIP 86—Marwick Codex 21

This third example of an amulet book came in a tooled leather pouch that was sealed and had to be cut open for study, indicating very clearly the function of the book as amulet rather than as a book to be read. The content of this 19th/20th century codex is *Prayer against the Tongue of People*.

148 · *Ethiopian Scribal Practice 1*

Plate 95: EMIP 87 (Weiner Codex 4), ff. iv v(erso) and 1r

Plate 95: EMIP 87—Weiner Codex 4

The illumination on folio iv v(erso) provides a wonderful example of how an artist has taken an old theme and applied it to his own day. The iconic subject matter depicted in the illumination is an old and well-known one in Ethiopian tradition. It is called "The Striking of the Head" and depicts the suffering of Jesus from the crown of thorns and beating of the Roman soldiers. The traditional way of depicting an evil person in Ethiopian art is to show them in profile, showing only one eye, and the Roman soldiers are shown in this way. The interesting thing here is that our artist has signaled to us that the Roman soldiers are Italians (shape of the face, the moustaches, and the receding hairline). Two dated texts in the manuscript give us a pretty good idea of the time in which these illuminations were made. The first, on folio i v(erso), is the record of a settlement of a dispute over property, dated Ḥamle 24, 1930 EC (July 31, 1938 AD.). The second is the will of *Ǝmmahoy* Dässəta Azagä, dated 1933 EC (1940/1 AD) on folio ii r(ecto). These would date the production and early use of the book to right around the time of the Italian occupation of Ethiopia (1936–1941). The illumination on folio 166r shows the same artistic intent. That illumination is an example of the traditional iconic theme of the Resurrection of Jesus, raising Adam and Eve from the dead. This icon always shows Jesus harrowing Hell with a processional cross and Adam and Eve being raised to life. Occasionally, an evil person or two (showing one eye) are depicted as remaining in the ground. In this case, four Italian soldiers are shown remaining in the ground.

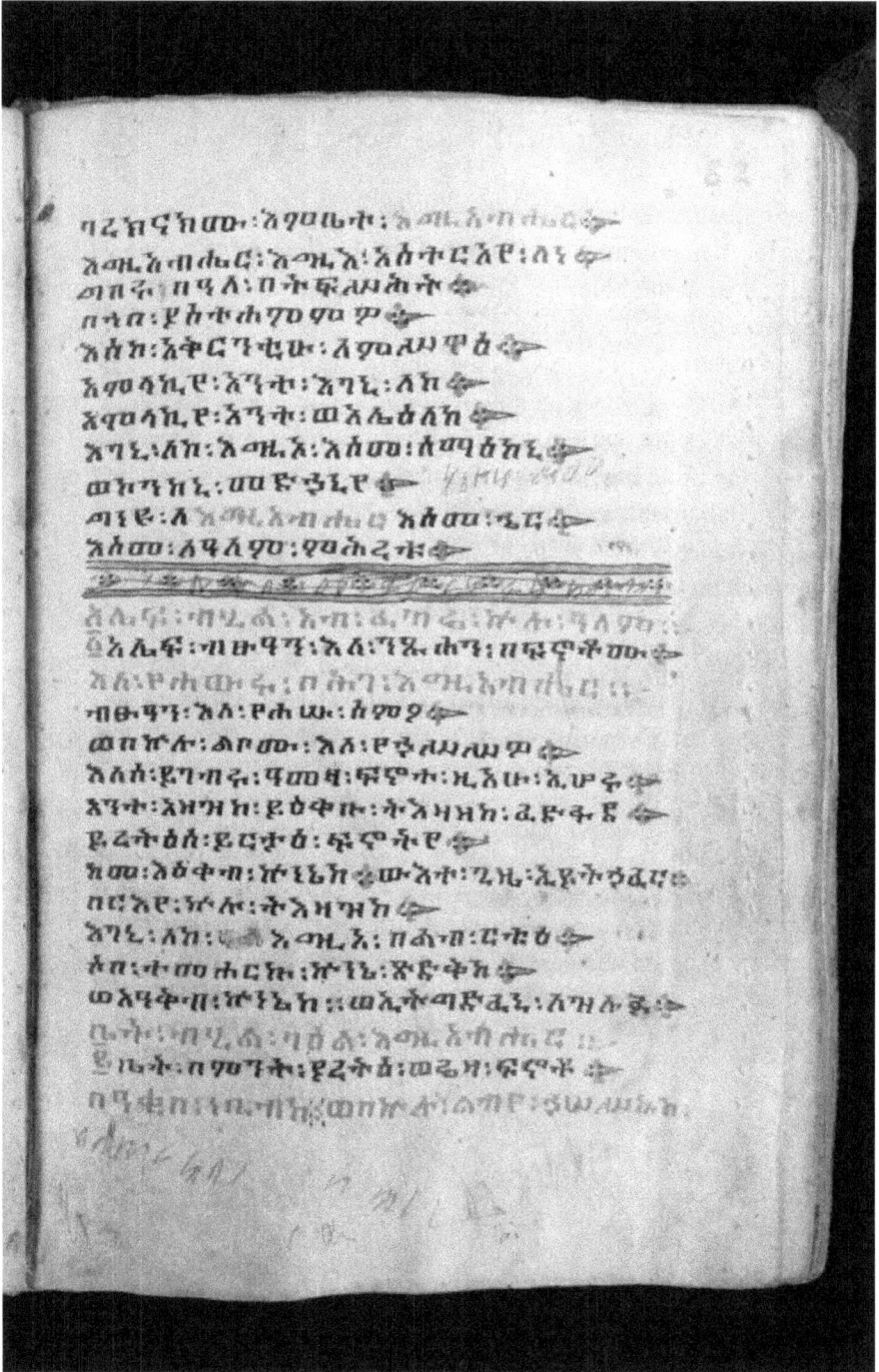

Plate 96: EMIP 88 (Weiner Codex 5), f. 80r

Plate 96: EMIP 88—Weiner Codex 5

In terms of layout and structure, the 118th psalm is perhaps the most interesting psalm in the Ethiopic tradition. The 151 Ethiopic psalms are ordered according to the numbering system in the Septuagint. The 118th Ethiopic psalm corresponds to the 119th in the Massoretic tradition. In Hebrew, this is one of the so-called acrostic psalms in which the successive lines of the psalm begin with the next letter of the Hebrew alphabet. The acrostic structure of Psalm 118 (=119) is all the more extraordinary since there are eight lines that begin with aleph, the first letter of the alphabet, then eight lines that begin with bet, the second letter, and so on. The Gəʽəz translators did not attempt to translate the psalm in such a way as to accomplish the same effect in their language. However, they were aware of the acrostic in Hebrew and had thought much about its significance in the Gəʽəz language. EMIP 88 is a good example of the various ways in which they dealt with this Psalm. In the first place, the psalm has been set off with its own ḥaräg, a treatment usually reserved for the first psalm of each section of 10 psalms. This particular device is rare in the Ethiopic tradition. The second, however is quite common. The psalm is divided into 22 sections corresponding to the 22 letters of the Hebrew alphabet. The normal way to signal this is to place a heading in red ink with a transliteration of the Hebrew letters at the top of each section. Occasionally, the sections will be marked with a succession of 22 numbers. This codex employs both devices. But, the most interesting aspect of the Ethiopic tradition at this point is the way in which they explore the spiritual meanings of the Hebrew letters. These explanations, often involving a pun with a word in the Gəʽəz language, are detailed in a line or two in red ink before the psalm itself begins. For instance, the first four letters are interpreted thus: "Aleph means Father (ʽb) the Creator of all the world;" "Bet means God is wealthy (ba ʽal);" "Gamel means God is wondrous (gərum);" and "Dalet means God is worthy (dəlləw)."

Plate 97: EMIP 89 (Weiner Codex 6), f. 68 (detail)

Plate 97: EMIP 89—Weiner 6

Plates 97 and 98 show details of a beautiful, 18th century copy of the Antiphonary for the Year, *Dəggʷa*. Several clues suggest that this manuscript was part of the Ethiopian Manuscript Microfilm Library project of the 1970's. Funded by the National Endowment for the Humanities, this project established a microfilm station in Addis Ababa. Over the course of several years almost 10,000 manuscripts were brought to the microfilm station and photographed. In preparation for filming, the manuscripts were foliated, often with stamped blue letters. Upon completion, the seal of the project was placed in a folio at the end of the manuscript. This plate shows a closeup of a stamped folio number that has been painted over by the "speckled garment artist." In addition, the inset shows the final folio of the codex, folio 113. A portion of the folio has been cut out of the manuscript.

154 · *Ethiopian Scribal Practice 1*

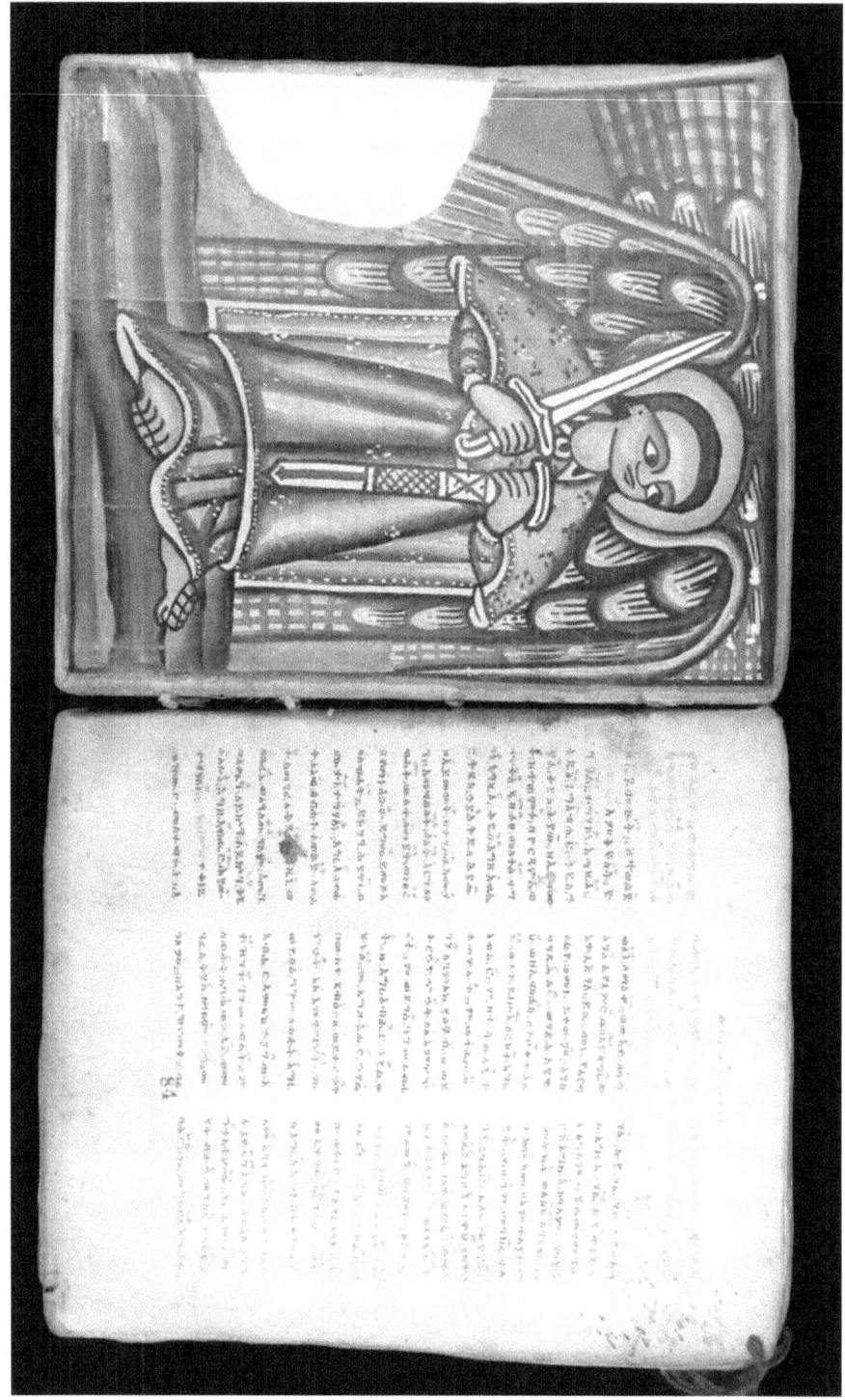

Plate 98: EMIP 89 (Weiner Codex 6), ff. 83v–84r

Plate 98: EMIP 89—Weiner 6

EMIP 89 is an 18th century Antiphonary for the Year (*Dəgg^{w}a*). This plate shows the beginning of the second major section at folio 84r: *Mə 'raf* chants. Notice that the text of the first three lines of each column is written in red ink. On the left we can see yet another example of the work of the "speckled garment artist." A piece of brown yarn has been sewn into the fore edge of folio 84 to mark the location of the illumination. On the right, we can also see an example of the stamped folio number "84" near the lower fore edge of the folio.

156 · *Ethiopian Scribal Practice 1*

Plate 99: EMIP 90 (Weiner 7), ff. 8v–9r, gutter

Plate 100: EMIP 91 (Weiner 8), exterior

Plate 99: EMIP 90—Weiner 7

Almost none of the manuscripts digitized in the project have seen the inside of a conservation laboratory. They carry the dirt and straw and bugs that became trapped within. We have taken care to photograph examples of some of the bugs and vegetation that are in the books, as this plate shows.

Plate 100: EMIP 91—Weiner 8

is another example of an accordion-fold book. This 20th-century book of *asmat* prayers is fairly small (90 x 75 x 22 mm) and was probably intended to serve as an amulet book for Wälättä Iyyäsus, its female owner (f. 11v). The subject matter of the *asmat* prayers all have to do with success in conception and deliverance from hemorrhage during childbirth.

158 · *Ethiopian Scribal Practice 1*

Plate 101: EMIP 92 (Weiner 9), panels 1 and 2

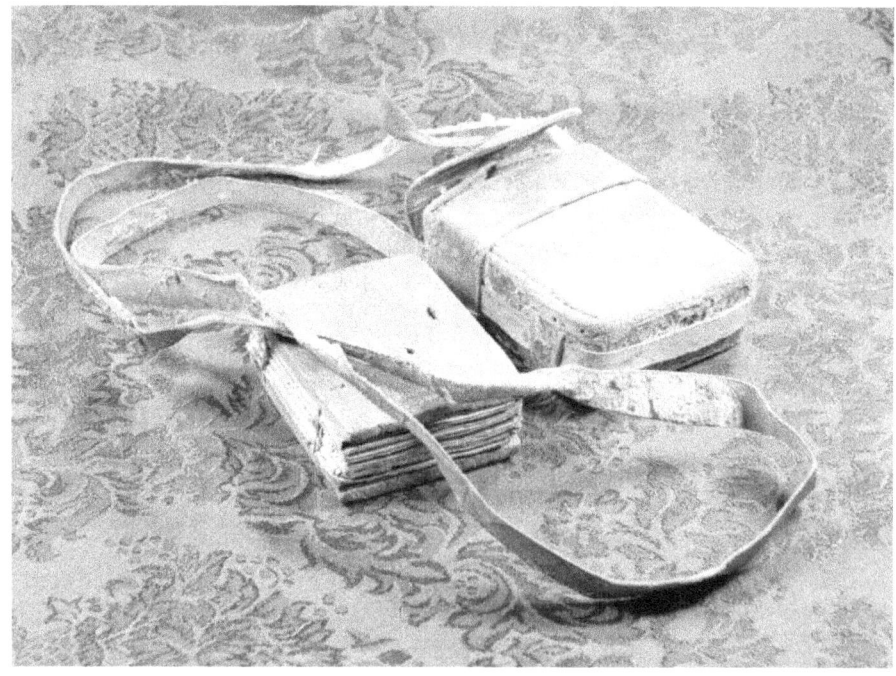

Plate 102: EMIP 93 (Marwick 23), codex and *maḫdar*

Plate 101: EMIP 92—Weiner 9

was produced by the same scribe as EMIP 91. It shares the same format (accordion-fold book), general dimensions (85 x 75 x 27 mm), materials, layout and scribal hand. It was no doubt intended as an amulet book to provide healing and protection to the wearer. In this case, the *asmat* prayers are directed toward protection from the evil eye and other evil spirits.

Plate 102: EMIP 93—Marwick Codex 23

This late-19th century codex is an example of the quintessential amulet book, the *Bandlet of Righteousness* (*Ləfafä Ṣədq*). The carrying case for this book has been preserved along with the small codex (75 x 58 x 24) which protected its wearer, Wälättä Śəllase (f. 23r and *passim*). The *Bandlet of Righteousness* tells the story of how Jesus conveyed to Mary the knowledge of the secret names of God.

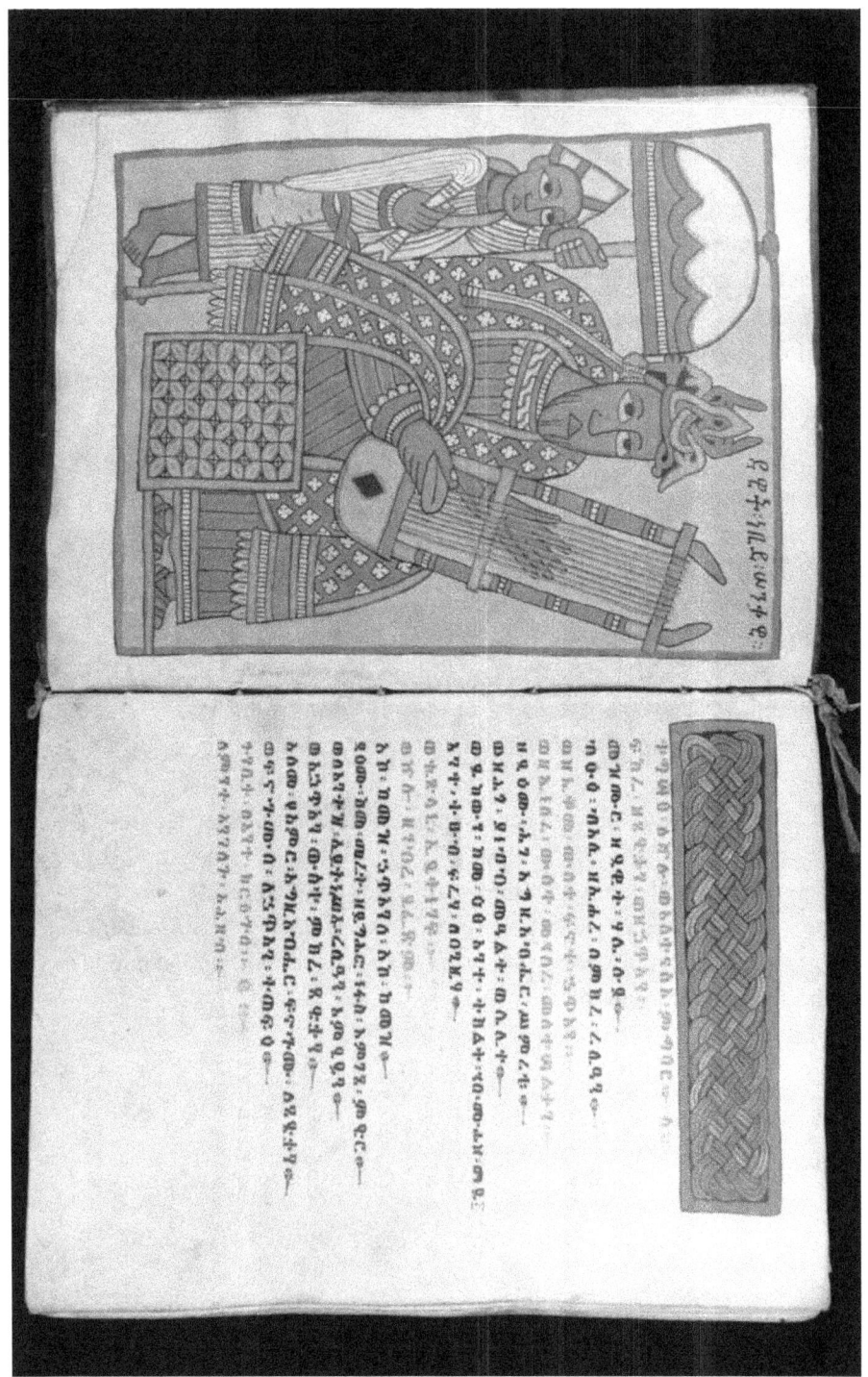

Plate 103: EMIP 94 (Weiner Codex 10), ff. ii v(erso)–1r

Plate 103: EMIP 94—Weiner Codex 10

This 20th century Psalter has many of the characteristics of a deluxe codex. One such characteristic is the large dimensions of the codex, 262 x 192 x 75 mm. This plate shows the generous margins, the beautiful and elaborate harägoč,[18] and the fine illuminations, all of which appear to be part of the original production of the book.

---

[18] Assefa (*PPM*, p. 264) confirms the correlation between number of *harägoč* and the cost of the manuscript. Specifically, he says that, around the turn from the nineteenth to the twentieth century, a Psalter with one *haräg* would cost twenty Maria Thersa dollars, but that one with 15 *harägoč* would cost fifty (p. 267). For more on the production of harägoč, see *MP Bookmaking*, p. 15. Sergew (*BIE*, pp. 34-35, cites from manuscripts in European libraries several colophons which tell the price of the manuscript.

162 · *Ethiopian Scribal Practice 1*

Plate 104: EMIP 94 (Weiner Codex 11), characteristics of deluxe codex

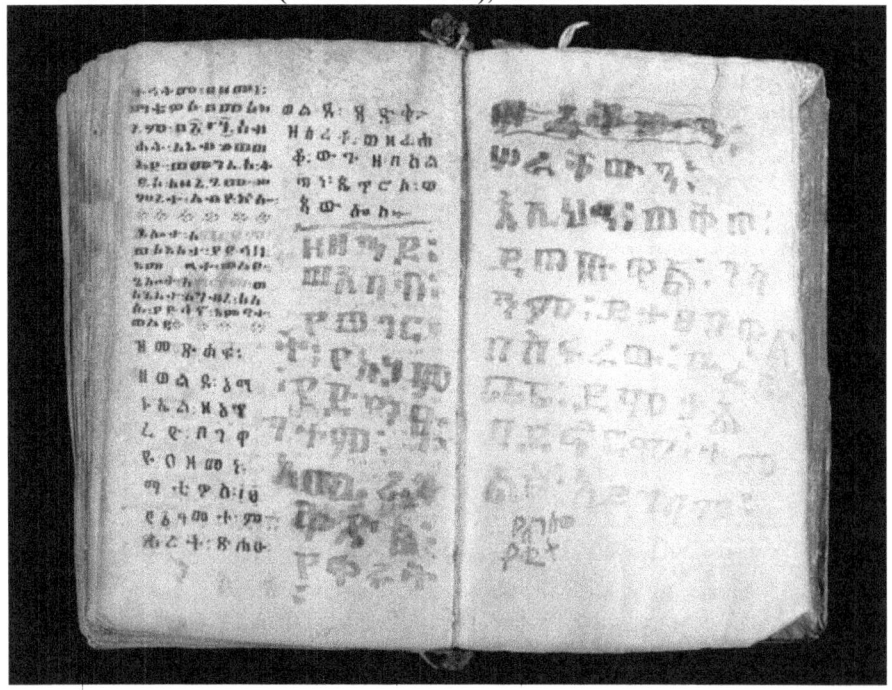

Plate 105: EMIP 95 (Weiner Codex 11), ff. 174v–175r

Plate 104: EMIP (Weiner Codex 10).

This plate shows several further features of the deluxe Ethiopic codex in the 20th century: a) an ornate full-stop symbol (written around 6,700 times in the first three works of the Psalter!); b) fabric lining to the inside covers; c) a three-quarter binding in tooled leather; d) ornate quire numbers; and e) finely executed head band and tail band.

Plate 105: EMIP 95—Weiner Codex 11

This plate shows the end of the final work in a standard Psalter, Gate of Light. Copied in the late-19th century, the book was purchased by Wäldä Amanu'el and his wife Wälättä Śəllase in the Ethiopian month of Gənbot, 1901 EC, which corresponds to May/June, 1909 C.E. The record of the purchase of the book appears copied in a trained hand in folio 174v, beginning half way down column one and ending at the top of column two. Following that, and continuing for six more folios in a crude hand, is a series of medical prescriptions against python and snake bite (ff. 174v–175r), against evil eye (ff. 175v–176r), for headache (f. 176v), for a person whom the enemy shut up (ff. 176rv), and a directive for what to do when an enemy rises.

Plate 106: EMIP 96 (Weiner Codex 12), front cover

Plate 107: EMIP 97 (Weiner Codex 13), ff. 40v–41r

Plate 106: EMIP 96—Weiner Codex 12

This early-19th century Psalter is bound in tooled leather. According to Mellors and Parsons (*MP Bookmaking*, p. 17), there are seven basic designs to the patterns on the finishing tools: the cross, horizontal lines, circles or dove's eye, crescent, criss-cross, palm shape, and a wave form.

Plate 107: EMIP 97—Weiner Codex 13

Despite the fact that it is now stored in a single-slip case, this 19th century Psalter has suffered damage from water which has caused the ink around the fore edge to run. Interestingly the damage is limited to folios 16–68. This plate also shows a nice example of a *ḫaräg* at the head of folio 41r, marking the beginning of the section of ten psalms beginning at chapter 51. In the top margin, written in dark pencil, we see the name of Gäbrä Iyyäsus that appears here, as well as on folios 15r, 23r, 33r and elsewhere.

Plate 108: EMIP 98 (Abilene Christian University Codex 1), f. 30v

Plate 109: EMIP 99 (Abilene Christian University Codices 1 and 2)

Plate 108: EMIP 98—Abilene Christian University Codex 1

This 19th century codex, containing the Prayer of Mary at Golgotha, shows an example of a different sort of damage. The top edges of this folio and the one prior to it have been nibbled by an animal.

Plate 109: EMIP 99—Abilene Christian University Codices 1 and 2

This plate gives an idea of the relative sizes of Ethiopic codices. The one on top (ACU Codex 1) measures 82 x 64 x 23 millimeters. Both in terms of size and content the manuscript seems intended for private use and would have been easy to transport and read in most any setting. Its small size may even indicate an intended use as an amulet. In contrast, the dimensions of the codex on the bottom are 235 x 205 x 82 millimeters. These dimensions, the sumptuous leather work on the exterior, the generous margins and large letters all suggest a deluxe manuscript in an ecclesial setting. This 17th century Psalter has two additional features that are out of the ordinary for Psalters. First, the margins to the Psalms are filled with annotations and commentary (see plate 110 below). Second, the content of the Psalms is not limited to the 151 psalms of David. At the end of each of the psalms of David is a corresponding psalm of the Virgin, *Mäzmurä Dəngəl*. These additional features suggest an ecclesial setting in which the manuscript would have served the liturgical and teaching functions carried out within a community. Such a manuscript would have retained its value for generations. On folio 158r (at the end of the psalms) is a record of sale of the manuscript between two priests: *Qes* Kənfe Wäd(d)i to *Qes* Ankore.

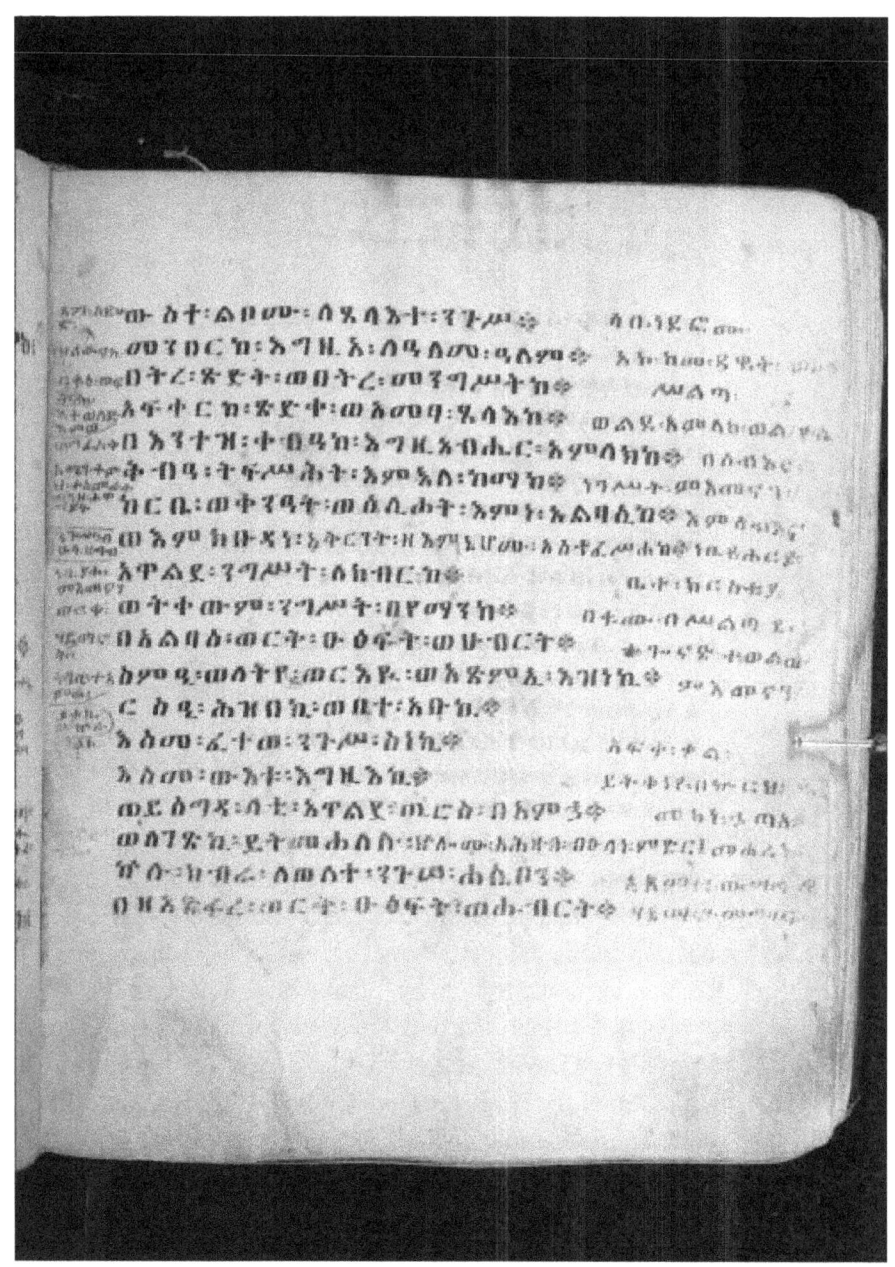

Plate 110: EMIP 99 (Abilene Christian University Codex 2), f. 46r

Plate 110: EMIP 99—Abilene Christian University Codex 2

This seventeenth-century Psalter contains hundreds of marginal notes. The purpose of these notes is to connect the readings of the text with the body of traditional interpretation created by Ethiopian scholars and known as the *Andemta*. This body of interpretation is vast and exists mostly in oral form. Students of the *Andemta* work very hard to master the memorization of the interpretations. When successful, they need only a verbal stimulus to trigger their memory of the interpretation. The marginal notes in the manuscript provide just such a stimulus.

    Each reading in the Psalm is said to contain a *meleket*, a symbol. The commentary which was memorized by the student will successfully explain the symbol; the student need only be pointed in the right direction. The marginal note provides the mnemonic which prompts the student to begin recitation.

    For instance, at Psalm 45:7b (ET), the text says, "Because of this, God, your Lord, has anointed you. . . ." The marginal note says, "Holy Spirit" and points the student toward the heart of the *andemta*. Where the text continues "with the oil of gladness beyond your companions" the marginal note indicates "miracles and wonders." Similarly, Psalm 45:6 says, "Your throne, O God, endures forever and ever." The margin says, "Your existence." Psalm 456b–47a says, "Your royal scepter is a scepter of equity; You love righteousness and hate wickedness." The marginal note prompts the reader that the text is about "His righteousness and justice." And where the text mentions myrrh, the marginal note points in the direction of a Christological interpretation: "about the entombment of his death."

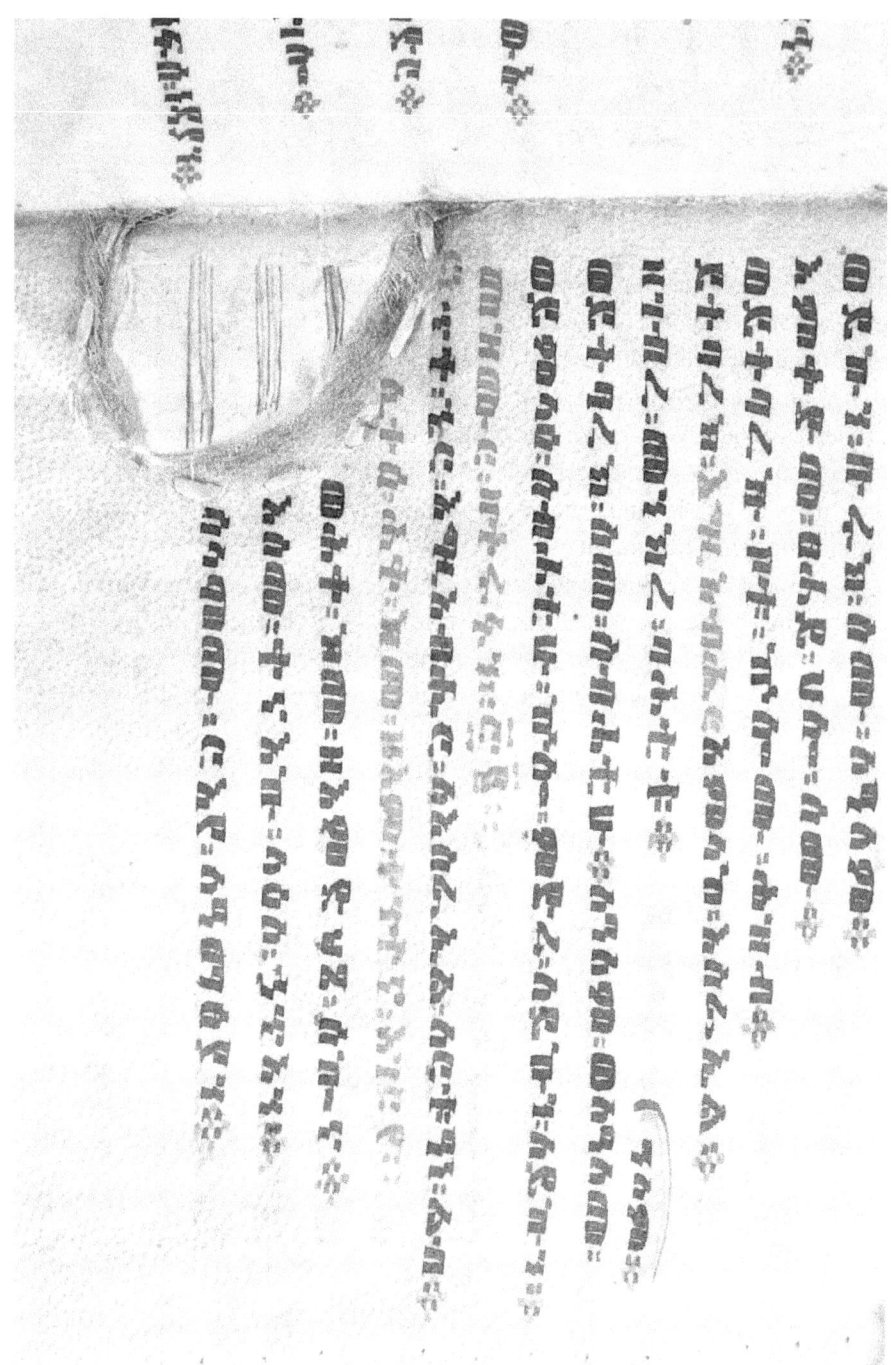

Plate 111: EMIP 100 (Weiner Codex 14), f. 59r

Plate 111: EMIP 100—Weiner Codex 14

The number and extent of repairs to the raw materials of a manuscript may indicate something about the scarceness of resources available to a scribe or in a region at a particular time. It is sometimes remarkable the lengths to which a scribe will go to render pieces of parchment useable in a manuscript. The sheet comprised of folios 54 and 59 had a large hole its center. This plate shows that the scribe has spliced a patch into the hole and marked off the portion which is not to be used for text. Other sheets in this 19th century Psalter contain similar dramatic repairs and defects in the materials: stitches to large tears (ff. 16/19, 24, 29, 81, and 115); unrepaired holes (ff. 57, 59, 64, 70, 79, 89, 121, 126, and 128); and uneven or undersized folios (ff. 74, 95, 127, 148, and 154). In addition, this manuscript employs several half sheets for folios 63, 66, 121, 137, 152, and 155 (i.e., a half sheet is visible on the other side of the quire). Other characteristics of the raw materials speak to the level of workmanship in the preparation of the parchment, for instance, the evenness or unevenness of the parchment, and the degree to which the hair follicles still show on the hair side of the parchment and the degree to which fat deposits still show on the skin side of the parchment). These characteristics combine to show a fairly low level of workmanship in this manuscript.

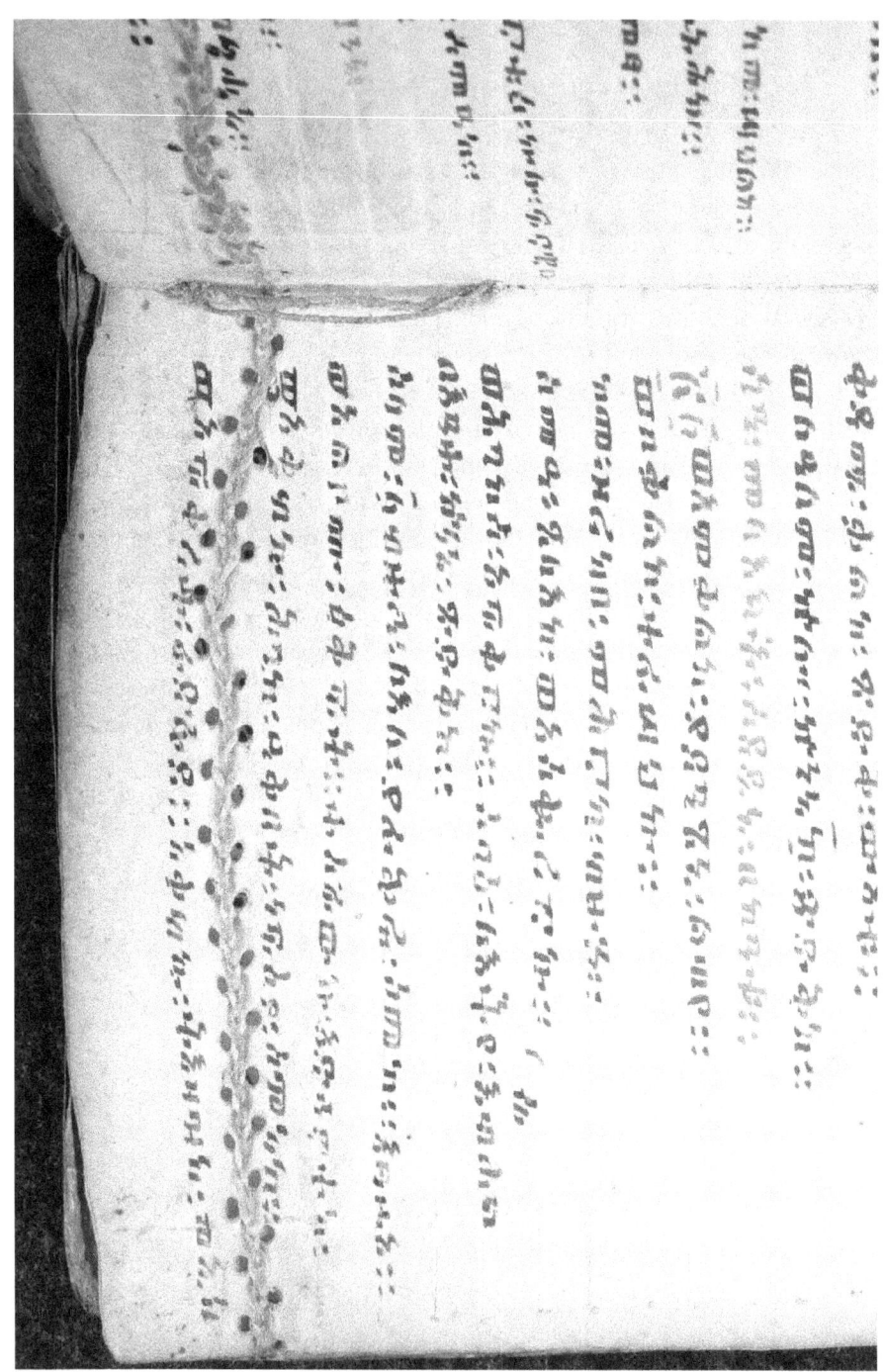

Plate 112: EMIP 101 (Weiner Codex 15), f. 112r

Plate 112: EMIP 101—Weiner Codex 15

The layout of the text block on a sheet of parchment is very standardized in the Ethiopic manuscript tradition. The characteristic that is most uniform is the relative sizes of the margins: the gutter margin is always smallest, the top and fore edge margins are fairly close to one another in size and are slightly larger than the gutter margin, and the bottom margin is always the largest. This 19th century Psalter has been trimmed along the bottom of the codex (presumably to fit a new set of board covers). That this was done after the book was produced is made clear by the number of folios that have the bottom line of text partially cut off (visible at ff. 16r, 29r, 43r, etc.). Another indicator of the trimming of the manuscript is to be seen in the location of the binding strings on the spine. The relative location of these binding strings is likewise uniform in the tradition: evenly spaced from top to bottom on the spine. In this plate we can see not only the dramatic repair of the parchment along the bottom of this sheet. We can also see the small bottom margin and the abnormal location (too low) of the binding strings in the gutter.

Plate 113: EMIP 102 (Weiner Codex 16), f. 73v

Plate 114: EMIP 103 (Weiner Codex 17), f. 19r

Plate 113: EMIP 102—Weiner Codex 16

A few of the manuscripts have seals or stamps of ownership somewhere in the codex. This 18th century Homiliary in Honor of the Monthly Feast of the Archangel Michael shows a seal on f. 73v. The stamp appears also on ff. 53v and 54r. Unfortunately, none of the seal impressions is clear enough to read all of the details.

Plate 114: EMIP 103—Weiner Codex 17

This 20th century Miracles of Jesus manuscript has thirty-seven illuminations. Some of them contain thematic elements that stem from the domain of the magical genres. This particular theme, containing a face in the middle of a multi-point star, is very common in scrolls of spiritual healing.

Plate 115: EMIP 104 (Weiner Codex 18), *maḥdär* and codex

Plate 116: EMIP 105 (Weiner Codex 19), f. 97r

Plate 115: EMIP 104—Weiner Codex 18

This 19th century manuscript contains the works Images of Mary (ff. 3r–15v), Jesus Christ (ff. 15v–30r), Arägawi/Zä-Mika'el (ff. 30r–37v), Gäbrä Mänfäs Qəddus (ff. 37v–42r), Michael (ff. 42r–52v), Gabriel (ff. 52v–59v) and George (ff. 59v–60v). It is kept in this neatly-fashioned case that incorporates colorful fabric into the carrying strap. We can also notice in this image the use of the non-traditional wide-grained wood for the cover.

Plate 116: EMIP 105—Weiner Codex 19

This 19th century codex contains the Book of Hours of *Abba* Giyorgis. Three illuminations have been added to the book. The one here depicts a story, recounted in the collection of Miracles of Mary, about a man with a stone foot, *Zä'ənb Ǝgru*, who entreats Mary to heal him.

List of the Manuscripts by EMIP and Owner Number

EMIP 1 = Herron Codex
EMIP 2 = Eliza Codex 1
EMIP 3 = Eliza Codex 2
EMIP 4 = Eliza Codex 3
EMIP 5 = Marwick Codex 1
EMIP 6 = Marwick Codex 2
EMIP 7 = Marwick Codex 3
EMIP 8 = Marwick Codex 4
EMIP 9 = Marwick Codex 5
EMIP 10 = Marwick Codex 6
EMIP 11 = Marwick Codex 7
EMIP 12 = Marwick Codex 8
EMIP 13 = Marwick Codex 9
EMIP 14 = Marwick Codex 10
EMIP 15 = Marwick Codex 11
EMIP 16 = Marwick Codex 12
EMIP 17 = Marwick Codex 13
EMIP 18 = Marwick Codex 14
EMIP 19 = Marwick Codex 15
EMIP 20 = Marwick Codex 16
EMIP 21 = Marwick Codex 17
EMIP 22 = Marwick Codex 18
EMIP 23 = Marwick Codex 19
EMIP 24 = Marwick Codex 20
EMIP 25 = Eliza Codex 4
EMIP 26 = Eliza Codex 5
EMIP 27 = Eliza Codex 6
EMIP 28 = Eliza Codex 7
EMIP 29 = Whisnant Codex 1
EMIP 30 = Whisnant Codex 2
EMIP 31 = Earl Codex
EMIP 32 = Delamarter Codex 1
EMIP 33 = Eliza Codex 8
EMIP 34 = Eliza Codex 9
EMIP 35 = Eliza Codex 10
EMIP 36 = Eliza Codex 11
EMIP 37 = Eliza Codex 12
EMIP 38 = Eliza Codex 13
EMIP 39 = Eliza Codex 14
EMIP 40 = Eliza Codex 15
EMIP 41 = Eliza Codex 16
EMIP 42 = Eliza Codex 17
EMIP 43 = Eliza Codex 18
EMIP 44 = Eliza Codex 19
EMIP 45 = Eliza Codex 20
EMIP 46 = Eliza Codex 21
EMIP 47 = Eliza Codex 22
EMIP 48 = Eliza Codex 23
EMIP 49 = Eliza Codex 24
EMIP 50 = Eliza Codex 25
EMIP 51 = Eliza Codex 26
EMIP 52 = Eliza Codex 27
EMIP 53 = Eliza Codex 28
EMIP 54 = Eliza Codex 29
EMIP 55 = Trinity Western University Eth. Ms. 1
EMIP 56 = Trinity Western University Eth. Ms. 2
EMIP 57 = Trinity Western University Eth. Ms. 3
EMIP 58 = Tsunami Codex
EMIP 59 = Kahan Codex
EMIP 60 = Eliza Codex 30
EMIP 61 = Eliza Codex 31
EMIP 62 = Eliza Codex 32
EMIP 63 = Eliza Codex 33
EMIP 64 = Eliza Codex 34
EMIP 65 = Eliza Codex 35
EMIP 66 = Eliza Codex 36
EMIP 67 = Focanti Codex 1

EMIP 68 = Focanti Codex 2
EMIP 69 = Focanti Codex 3
EMIP 70 = Marwick Codex 22
EMIP 71 = University of Oregon Museum of Natural and Cultural History, 10–845
EMIP 72 = University of Oregon Museum of Natural and Cultural History, 10–843
EMIP 73 = University of Oregon Museum of Natural and Cultural History, 10–844
EMIP 74 = Mount Angel Codex 46
EMIP 75 = Weiner Codex 1
EMIP 76 = Weiner Codex 2
EMIP 77 = Bernhardt Codex
EMIP 78 = Eliza Codex 37
EMIP 79 = Eliza Codex 38
EMIP 80 = Eliza Codex 39
EMIP 81 = Eliza Codex 40
EMIP 82 = Eliza Codex 41
EMIP 83 = Weiner Codex 3
EMIP 84 = Delamarter Codex 2
EMIP 85 = Trinity Western University Eth. Ms. 4
EMIP 86 = Marwick Codex 21
EMIP 87 = Weiner Codex 4
EMIP 88 = Weiner Codex 5
EMIP 89 = Weiner Codex 6
EMIP 90 = Weiner Codex 7
EMIP 91 = Weiner Codex 8
EMIP 92 = Weiner Codex 9
EMIP 93 = Marwick Codex 23
EMIP 94 = Weiner Codex 10
EMIP 95 = Weiner Codex 11
EMIP 96 = Weiner Codex 12
EMIP 97 = Weiner Codex 13
EMIP 98 = Abilene Christian University Codex 1
EMIP 99 = Abilene Christian University Codex 2
EMIP 100 = Weiner Codex 14
EMIP 101 = Weiner Codex 15
EMIP 102 = Weiner Codex 16
EMIP 103 = Weiner Codex 17
EMIP 104 = Weiner Codex 18
EMIP 105 = Weiner Codex 19

List of Dated or Datable Manuscripts

1706–8 (reign of Täklä Haymanot I): EMIP 72
1720–1743 (reign of Metropolitan Krestodolu): EMIP 46
1747–1761 (reign of Iyyo'as): EMIP 20
1770–1803 (reign of Metropolitan Yosab): EMIP 27
1855–1868 (reign of Tewodros): EMIP 43
1872–1889 (reign of Yoḥannəs IV): EMIP 81
1889–1926 (reign of Metropolitan Matewos): EMIP 77
1923: January 29 (Ṭərr 21, 1915): EMIP 11
1923/24 (1916 EC): EMIP 37
1928–1942 (reign of Patriarch Yoḥannəs XIX): EMIP 80, 82
1940: November 5 (Ṭəqəmt 27, 1933 EC): EMIP 31
1930–1974 (reign of Haile Sellasie): EMIP 59
2000: December 2 (Ḫədar 23, 1993EC): EMIP 38

List of Undated and Composite Manuscripts

16th Century
  16th century: EMIP 15 (composite), and 42 (composite)
17th Century
  17th century: EMIP 57 and 99
  Late 17th century: EMIP 1, 12, and 19
18th Century
  Early 18th century: EMIP 13, 18, and 24
  18th century: EMIP 2, 6, 9, 29, 30, 34, 42 (composite), 53, 60, 66, 68, 69, 83, 89, and 102
  Late 18th century: EMIP 7, and 33 (composite)
  18th/19th century: EMIP 64
19th Century
  Early 19th century: EMIP 21, 36, and 96
  19th century: EMIP 8, 14, 10 (composite), 15 (composite), 16, 23, 33 (composite), 35, 39, 45, 50, 56 (composite), 67, 76, 78, 97, 98, 100, 101, 104, and 105
  Late 19th century: EMIP 28, 93, and 95
  19th/20th century: EMIP 5, 40, 51, 52, 54, 55, 58, 62, 75, and 86
20th Century
  Early 20th century: EMIP 48, and 65
  20th century: EMIP 4, 10 (composite), 17, 22, 25, 26, 41, 47, 49, 56 (composite), 61, 63, 70, 71, 73, 74, 79, 85, 87, 88, 90, 91, 92, 94, and 103
  Late 20th century: EMIP 3, 32, 37 (composite), 44, and 84

For Further Reading

Arabic Manuscript Tradition

Baker, Colin F. *Qur'an Manuscripts: Calligraphy, Illumination, Design.* London: British Library, 2007.

Arberry, A. J. *The Koran Illuminated; A Handlist of the Korans in the Chester Beatty Library.* Dublin: Hodges, Figgis, 1967.

Armenian Manuscript Tradition

Der Nersessian, Sirarpie. The Chester Beatty Library: A Catalogue of the Armenian Manuscripts. Dublin, 1958.

Der Nersessian, Sirarpie. *Armenian Manuscripts in the Walters Art Gallery.* Baltimore: The Trustees, 1973.

Dimitrova, Ekaterina. *The Gospels of Tsar Ivan Alexander.* London: British Library, 1994.

Mathews, Thomas F., and Alice Taylor. *The Armenian Gospels of Gladzor: The Life of Christ Illuminated.* Los Angeles: J. Paul Getty Museum, 2001.

Nersessian, Vrej. *Armenian Illuminated Gospel-Books.* London: British Library, 1987.

Nersessian, Vrej. *The Bible in the Armenian Tradition.* Los Angeles, California: J. Paul Getty Museum, 2001.

Stone, Nira, and Michael E. Stone. *The Armenians: Art, Culture and Religion.* Dublin: The Chester Beatty Library, 2007.

Ethiopian Art

Chojnacki, Stanisław. 2004. "Ethiopian Warrior Saints in 18th-Century Miniatures and Their Significance in the Cultural History of Ethiopia". *Indigenous and the Foreign in Christian Ethiopian Art: on Portuguese-Ethiopian Contacts in the 16th–17th Centuries: Papers from the Fifth International Conference on the History of Ethiopian Art (Arrabida, 26–30 November 1999).* 73–82.

Di Salvo, Mario, Stanisław Chojnacki, and Osvaldo Raineri. *Churches of Ethiopia: The Monastery of Nārgā Śellāsē.* Milano, Italy: Skira Editore, 1999.

Heldman, Marilyn Eiseman, S. C. Munro-Hay, and Roderick Grierson. *African Zion: The Sacred Art of Ethiopia.* New Haven: Yale University Press, 1993.

International Conference on the History of Ethiopian Art, Manuel João Ramos, and Isabel Boavida. *The Indigenous and the Foreign in Christian Ethiopian Art: On Portuguese-Ethiopian Contacts in the 16th–17th Centuries : Papers from the Fifth International Conference on the History of Ethiopian Art (Arrabida, 26–30 November 1999)*. [Lisbon, Portugal]: Calouste Gulbenkian Foundation, 2004.

Mercier, Jacques. *Ethiopian Magic Scrolls*. New York: G. Braziller, 1979.

Silverman, Raymond Aaron, Qēs Adamu Tesfaw, Leah Niederstadt, and N. W. Sobania. *Painting Ethiopia: The Life and Work of Qes Adamu Tesfaw*. Los Angeles: UCLA Fowler Museum of Cultural History, 2005.

Ethiopian Manuscript Tradition and General

Gervers, Michael. 2004. "The Portuguese Import of Luxury Textiles to Ethiopia in the 16th and 17th Centuries and Their Subsequent Artistic Influence". *Indigenous and the Foreign in Christian Ethiopian Art: on Portuguese-Ethiopian Contacts in the 16th–17th Centuries: Papers from the Fifth International Conference on the History of Ethiopian Art (Arrabida, 26–30 November 1999)*. 121–134.

Hammerschmidt, Ernst. *Studies in the Ethiopic Anaphoras*. Äthiopistische Forschungen, Bd. 25. Stuttgart: F. Steiner Verlag Wiesbaden, 1988.

Henze, Martha. 2004. "Imported Textiles in Ethiopian Traditions". *Indigenous and the Foreign in Christian Ethiopian Art: on Portuguese-Ethiopian Contacts in the 16th–17th Centuries: Papers from the Fifth International Conference on the History of Ethiopian Art (Arrabida, 26–30 November 1999)*. 135–145.

Knibb, Michael A. *Translating the Bible: The Ethiopic Version of the Old Testament*. The Schweich lectures of the British Academy, 1995. Oxford: Published for The British Academy by Oxford University Press, 1999.

Manley, Deborah, and Peta Rée. *Henry Salt: Artist, Traveller, Diplomat, Egyptologist*. London: Libri, 2001.

Pearce, Nathaniel, William Coffin, and John James Halls. *The Life and Adventures of Nathaniel Pearce*. London: Henry Colburn and Richard Bentley, 1831.

Stoffregen Pedersen, Kirsten. *Traditional Ethiopian Exegesis of the Book of Psalms*. Wiesbaden: Harrassowitz, 1995.

Ullendorff, Edward. *Ethiopia and the Bible*. The Schweich lectures, 1967. London: published for the British Academy by the Oxford U.P., 1968.

Zuurmond, Rochus. *Novum testamentum Aethiopice. general introduction. The synoptic gospels*. Äthiopistische Forschungen, Bd. 27. Wiesbaden: Harrassowitz, 1989.

Ethiopian Scribal Practice

Assefa Liben, "Preparation of Parchment Manuscripts." *Bulletin of Ethnological Museum, University College of Addis Ababa*, 8 (1958) pp. 254–267.

Mellors, John and Anne Parsons. *Scribes of South Gondar*. London: New Cross Books, 2002.

Mellors, John and Anne Parsons. *Ethiopian Bookmaking*. London: New Cross Books, 2002.

O'Hanlon, Douglas. *Features of the Abyssinian Church*. London: SPCK, 1946.

Sergew Hable Selassie, *Bookmaking in Ethiopia*. Leiden: Karstens Drukkers, 1981.

Uhlig, Siegbert. *Introduction to Ethiopian Palaeography*. Äthiopistische Forschungen, Bd. 28. Stuttgart: F. Steiner, 1990.

General, Scribal Practice and Illuminations

Alexander, J. J. G. *The Decorated Letter*. New York: G. Braziller, 1978.

Alexander, J. J. G. *Medieval Illuminators and Their Methods of Work*. New Haven: Yale University Press, 1992.

Avrin, Leila. *Scribes, Script, and Books: The Book Arts from Antiquity to the Renaissance*. Chicago: American Library Association, 1991.

Bradley, John William. *Illuminated Manuscripts*. Little books on art. London: Methuen, 1905.

Brown, Michelle. *Understanding Illuminated Manuscripts: A Guide to Technical Terms*. Malibu, California: J. Paul Getty Museum in association with the British Library, 1994.

Brown, Michelle. *In the Beginning: Bibles Before the Year 1000*. Washington, D.C.: Freer Gallery of Art and Arthur M. Sackler Gallery, Smithsonian Institution, 2006.

De Hamel, Christopher. *Scribes and Illuminators*. Medieval craftsmen. Toronto: University of Toronto Press, 1992.

De Hamel, Christopher. *A History of Illuminated Manuscripts*. London: Phaidon Press, 1994.

De Hamel, Christopher. *The British Library Guide to Manuscript Illumination: History and Techniques*. Toronto: University of Toronto Press, 2001.

De Hamel, Christopher. *The Book: A History of the Bible*. London: Phaidon, 2001.

Didron, Adolphe Napoléon. *Christian Iconography; The History of Christian Art in the Middle Ages*. New York: F. Ungar Pub. Co, 1965.

Diringer, David. *The Book Before Printing: Ancient, Medieval, and Oriental*. New York: Dover Publications, 1982.

Fingernagel, Andreas, and Christian Gastgeber. *The Most Beautiful Bibles*. Hong Kong: Taschen, 2008.

Greenfield, Jane. *ABC of Bookbinding: A Unique Glossary with Over 700 Illustrations for Collectors & Librarians*. New Castle, DE: Oak Knoll Press, 1998.

Hourihane, Colum, and John Plummer. *Between the Picture and the Word: Manuscript Studies from the Index of Christian Art*. [Princeton, N.J.]: Index of Christian Art, Dept. of Art and Archaeology, Princeton University, 2005.

Hutchinson Edgar, David. *Treasuring the Word: An Introduction to Biblical Manuscripts in the Chester Beatty Library*. The Irish treasures series. Dublin: TownHouse, 2003.

Irvine, Martin. *The Making of Textual Culture: 'grammatica' and Literary Theory, 350–1100*. Cambridge studies in medieval literature, 19. Cambridge [England]: Cambridge University Press, 1994.

Kendrick, Laura. *Animating the Letter: The Figurative Embodiment of Writing from Late Antiquity to the Renaissance*. Columbus, Ohio: Ohio State University Press, 1999.

Kenyon, Frederic G. *Books and Readers in Ancient Greece and Rome*. Oxford: Clarendon Press, 1951.

Kilgour, Frederick G. *The Evolution of the Book*. New York: Oxford University Press, 1998.

Lockwood, Wilfrid. *The Word of God: Biblical Manuscripts at the Chester Beatty Library, Dublin*. Dublin: Chester Beatty Library, 1987.

Marks, P. J. M. *The British Library Guide to Bookbinding: History and Techniques*. Toronto: University of Toronto Press, 1998.

McKendrick, Scot, and Kathleen Doyle. *Bible Manuscripts: 1400 Years of Scribes and Scripture*. London: British Library, 2007.

Merian, Matthaeus. *Iconum Biblicarum*. Wenatchee, WA: AVB Press, 1981.
Miller, Stephen M., and Robert V. Huber. *The Bible: A History : the Making and Impact of the Bible*. Intercourse, PA: Good Books, 2004.
Page, Sophie. *Magic in Medieval Manuscripts*. Toronto: University of Toronto Press, 2004.
Pattie, T. S. *Manuscripts of the Bible*. London: British Library, 1979.
Reynolds, L. D., and Nigel Guy Wilson. *Scribes and Scholars: A Guide to the Transmission of Greek and Latin Literature*. Oxford: Clarendon Press, 1974.
Sharpe, John L., and Kimberly Van Kampen. *The Bible As Book: The Manuscript Tradition*. London: British Library, 1998.
Walther, Ingo F., and Norbert Wolf. *Codices Illustres: The World's Most Famous Illuminated Manuscripts 400–1600*. Köln: Taschen, 2001.
Weitzmann, Kurt. *Late Antique and Early Christian Book Illumination*. New York: G. Braziller, 1977.
Williams, John. *Imaging the Early Medieval Bible*. The Penn State series in the history of the book. University Park, Pa: Pennsylvania State University Press, 1999.

Greek Manuscript Tradition

Comfort, Philip Wesley. *Early Manuscripts & Modern Translations of the New Testament*. Wheaton, Ill: Tyndale House Publishers, 1990.
Elliott, J. K. *A Bibliography of Greek New Testament Manuscripts*. Society for New Testament Studies monograph series, 109. Cambridge: Cambridge University Press, 2005.
Finegan, Jack. *Encountering New Testament Manuscripts; A Working Introduction to Textual Criticism*. Grand Rapids, Michigan: Eerdmans, 1974.
Hatch, William Henry Paine. *Greek and Syrian Miniatures in Jerusalem, with an Introduction and a Description of Each of the Seventy–One Miniatures Reproduced*. Cambridge, Mass: Mediaeval academy of America, 1931.
Hurtado, Larry W. *The Freer Biblical Manuscripts: Fresh Studies of an American Treasure Trove*. Text-critical studies, v. 6. Atlanta, GA: Society of Biblical Literature, 2006.
Hurtado, Larry W. *The Earliest Christian Artifacts: Manuscripts and Christian Origins*. Grand Rapids, Michigan: William B. Eerdmans Pub. Co, 2006.

Jongkind, Dirk. *Scribal habits of Codex sinaiticus*. Piscataway, NJ: Gorgias Press, 2007.
Kenyon, Frederic G. *The Palaeography of Greek Papyri*. Oxford: Clarendon Press, 1899.
McKendrick, Scot, and Orlaith O'Sullivan. *The Bible As Book: The Transmission of the Greek Text*. London: British Library, 2003.
McKendrick, Scot. *In a Monastery Library: Preserving Codex Sinaiticus and the Greek Written Heritage*. London: British Library, 2006.
Metzger, Bruce Manning. *Manuscripts of the Greek Bible: An Introduction to Greek Palaeography*. New York: Oxford University Press, 1981.
Roberts, Colin H. *An Unpublished Fragment of the Fourth Gospel in the John Rylands Library*. Manchester: Manchester University Press [etc.], 1935.
Roberts, Colin H. *Manuscript, Society, and Belief in Early Christian Egypt*. London: published for the British Academy by Oxford University Press, 1979.
Turner, E. G. *The Papyrologist at Work*. Greek, Roman and Byzantine monographs, no. 6. Durham, N.C.: Duke University, 1973.

Hebrew Manuscript Tradition
Berkowitz, David Sandler. *In Remembrance of Creation; Evolution of Art and Scholarship in the Medieval and Renaissance Bible*. Waltham, Mass: Brandeis University Press, 1968.
Freedman, David Noel, K. A. Mathews, and Richard S. Hanson. *The Paleo-Hebrew Leviticus Scroll (11QpaleoLev)*. [Philadelphia, Pa.]: American Schools of Oriental Research, 1985.
Gold, Leonard Singer. *A Sign and a Witness: 2,000 Years of Hebrew Books and Illuminated Manuscripts*. Studies in Jewish history. New York: New York Public Library, 1988.
Gutmann, Joseph. *Hebrew Manuscript Painting*. New York: G. Braziller, 1978.
Herbert, Edward D., and Emanuel Tov. *The Bible As Book: The Hebrew Bible and the Judaean Desert Discoveries*. London: British Library ; New Castle, DE : Oak Knoll Press, 2002.
Jewish Museum (New York, N.Y.), R. Grafman, and Vivian B. Mann. *Crowning Glory: Silver Torah Ornaments of the Jewish Museum, New York*. New York: Jewish Museum, New York, under the auspices of the Jewish Theological Seminary of America, 1996.

Joel ben Simeon, Eleazar ben Judah, and David Goldstein. *The Ashkenazi Haggadah: A Hebrew Manuscript of the Mid-15th Century from the Collections of the British Library*. New York: H.N. Abrams, 1985.

Kelley, Page H., Daniel S. Mynatt, and Timothy G. Crawford. *The Masorah of Biblia Hebraica Stuttgartensia: Introduction and Annotated Glossary*. Grand Rapids, Michigan: W.B. Eerdmans, 1998.

Reif, Stefan C. *A Jewish Archive from Old Cairo: The History of Cambridge University's Genizah Collection*. Culture and civilisation in the Middle East. Richmond, Surrey: Curzon, 2000.

Spertus College of Judaica, and Norman Golb. *Spertus College of Judaica Yemenite Manuscripts*. Chicago: Spertus College of Judaica Press, 1972.

Strack, Hermann Leberecht. *The Hebrew Bible, Latter Prophets; The Babylonian Codex of Petrograd*. New York: KTAV Publishing House, 1971.

Tahan, Ilana. *Hebrew Manuscripts: The Power of Script and Image*. London: British Library, 2007.

Tov, Emanuel. *Scribal Practices and Approaches Reflected in the Texts Found in the Judean Desert*. Studies on the texts of the desert of Judah, v. 54. Leiden: Brill, 2004.

Yeivin, Israel. *Introduction to the Tiberian Masorah*. Masoretic studies, no. 5. Missoula, Mont: Published by Scholars Press for the Society of Biblical Literature and the International Organization for Masoretic Studies, 1980.

Latin Manuscript Tradition

Brown, Michelle. *Painted Labyrinth: The World of the Lindisfarne Gospels*. London: British Library, 2004.

Coen Pirani, Emma. *Gothic Illuminated Manuscripts*. Feltham: Hamlyn, 1970.

McNally, Robert E. *The Bible in the Early Middle Ages*. Woodstock papers; occasional essays for theology, no. 4. Westminster, Maryland: Newman Press, 1959.

Williams, John. *Early Spanish Manuscript Illumination*. New York: G. Braziller, 1977.

Samaritan Manuscript Tradition

Anderson, Robert T., and Terry Giles. *The Keepers: An Introduction to the History and Culture of the Samaritans.* Peabody, Mass: Hendrickson Publishers, 2002.

British Library, and Alan David Crown. *A Catalogue of the Samaritan Manuscripts in the British Library.* London: The Library, 1998.

Crown, Alan David. *Samaritan Scribes and Manuscripts.* Tübingen: Mohr Siebeck, 2001.

Syriac Manuscript Tradition

Brock, Sebastian P. *The Bible in the Syriac tradition.* Gorgias handbooks, v. 7. Piscataway, N.J.: Gorgias Press, 2006.

Brock, Sebastian P. *An Introduction to Syriac Studies.* Gorgias handbooks, v. 4. Piscataway, NJ: Gorgias Press, 2006.

Segal, J. B. *The Diacritical Point and the Accents in Syriac.* London oriental series, 2. London: Oxford University Press, 1953.

Index of Scribal Practices

Accordion-fold book, 127, 147, 157, 159
Amulet book, 145, 147, 157, 159
Arranged
    for the church calendar, 21
    for the days of the week, 5, 21, 113
    for the months of the year, 129
Binding, 45, 55, 173
Bridle attachment, 11, 27
Case, 2, 3, 41, 79, 117, 159, 165, 177
Chain stitches, 5, 9, 27, 33, 45, 81, 97, 101, 103
Colophon, 53
Colometric layout of text, 47, 85
Columns, 25, 73, 143, 155
Common (opposite of deluxe), 115
Cost of manuscript, 3
Covers
    boards, 9, 27, 37, 53, 73
    leather bound, 17, 39, 59, 91, 103, 127, 163, 165, 167
    linen cover, 63, 65, 117
    made off the book, 103
    wood, 97, 105, 135
Cryptogram, 117
Damage
    from animal, 167
    water, 141, 165
Deluxe manuscripts, 79, 103, 161
Ethiopian Manuscript Microfilm Library, 153
Fabric lined, 103, 127, 163
Folio
    layout of textblock, 43
    stubs, 63, 139, 171, 175

Forged paintings, 13, 15, 67, 71, 79, 81, 87, 93, 133, 141
Full-stop symbol, 19, 25, 31, 47, 51, 63, 83, 109, 123, 125, 163
Hair follicles in parchment, 121, 171
Half sheets, 139, 171
Haräg, 5, 7, 11, 19, 25, 31, 37, 53, 59, 65, 79, 83, 101, 107, 111, 137, 149, 161, 165
Headband and tailband, 2, 3, 5, 17, 27, 39, 79, 91, 103, 127, 163
Hinged linings, 103
Illuminations, 7, 15, 29, 67, 71, 79, 81, 87, 91, 93, 99, 107, 111, 129, 133, 135, 141, 149, 153, 155, 157, 159, 161, 175, 177
Insects, 157
Justified text, 51
King mentioned, 77, 103, 123
Layout of Psalter, 51, 59, 79, 83, 125, 151
Line of alternating red and black dots, 25, 49
Lined paper, 63
Lines of alternating red and black dots, 123
Lines per folio, 73, 103, 115
Marginal notes, 169
Margins, 79, 173
Margins justified, 25
Metropolitan mentioned, 81
Midpoint of the Psalms, 119
Mirror niche, 11
Musical notation, 11, 37, 45, 59, 123, 155
Name of scribe, 57
Note of ownership, 49, 143

Numbers, 53
Overlooked text, 113
Paleography, 35, 75, 81, 113, 125
Palindrome, 117
Patriarch mentioned, 141
Prickings, 43
Printed picture, 63
Psalter
   line of text too long, 51, 79
   spiritual meaning of the Hebrew letters in Psalm 118, 151
Quantity of parchment, 121
Quire construction, 19, 39, 139
Quire numbers, 19, 51, 55, 79, 133, 163
Quires, 89
Quires from varying sources, 73, 75, 89
Rebound book, 61, 73, 81, 97
Records and transactions, 57, 63, 93, 101, 115, 149, 163
Red ink, 5, 9, 69, 77, 85, 123, 131
   lines written entirely in red ink, 25, 29, 37, 59, 71, 75, 81, 83, 93, 101, 103, 123, 137, 143

Rejected leaf, 55
Repairs, 11, 33, 37, 41, 61, 73, 105, 109, 119, 121, 171, 173
   dry-stitch, 33, 119
   reinforcement strips, 41, 45, 61, 73
   splicing parchment, 109, 121
   wet-stitch, 33
Rhyming text, 31
Rubrication with alternating red and black letters, 69
Scoring, 43
Scribal education, 125
Scribal school, 95
Seal of ownership, 63, 175
Section divisions, 5, 25, 31
Social location of manuscripts, 57
Spine, 2, 3, 27, 39, 45, 61, 73, 97, 103
Spine strap, 135
String navigation system, 13, 45, 79, 81, 93, 141, 155
Time to copy manuscripts, 19
Tooled leather, 59, 79, 127, 145, 165, 167
Varia, 23

www.ingramcontent.com/pod-product-compliance
Lightning Source LLC
Chambersburg PA
CBHW080538300426
44111CB00017B/2793